HOW TO
PRAY
EFFECTIVELY

VOLUME ONE

understanding the rules of prayer for different situations
and how to apply them for your desired outcome

Chris Oyakhilome, PhD

HOW TO PRAY EFFECTIVELY (Vol.1)

...understanding the rules of prayer for different situations and how to apply them for your desired outcome.

ISBN 978-978-53088-0-8

All Scripture quotations are taken from the King James Version of the Bible unless otherwise indicated

BELIEVERS' LOVEWORLD INC.

a.k.a Christ Embassy

UNITED KINGDOM:
Christ Embassy Int'l Office
LoveWorld Conference Center
Cheriton High Street,
Folkestone, Kent CT19 4QJ
Tel:+44(0)1303 270970
Fax: 01303 274 372

CANADA:
101 Ross Dean Drive,
Toronto, ON, Canada M9L 1S6
Tel/Fax:+1-416-746 5080

USA:
Christ Embassy Houston
12400 Westheimer Road,
Houston, Texas 77077
Tel:+1-281-759-5111;
    +1-281-759-6218

NIGERIA:
LoveWorld Conference Center
Kudirat Abiola Way,
Oregun, Ikeja, Lagos
P.O. Box 13563 Ikeja,Lagos.
Tel: +234-8023324188,
    +234-8052464131,
    +234-1-8925724

SOUTH AFRICA:
303 Pretoria Avenue
Cnr. Harley and Bram Fischer,
Randburg, Gauteng
South Africa.
Tel: +27 11 3260971
    +27 11 3260972

email: cec@christembassy.org
website: www.christembassy.org

Contents

Introduction

$\mathcal{P}$rayer is primarily our communication with the Lord. Communication has purpose, and the purpose usually determines the mode and relevant details for the communication to be effective.

The disciples of Jesus were Jews and they knew how to pray religiously. After walking with Jesus for a while, they realized that Jesus didn't pray as they did. He actually had results continually in a way that startled them. They finally said to the Master, "Teach us to pray."

Many have had their understanding of prayer distorted by "religion" and wrong teaching. As a result, they have difficulties changing their misconceptions on even fundamental truths about prayer.

Why We Pray

Praying is such an important part of our lives as Christians. First of all, we must recognize prayer as a privilege as well as an honour. Every moment of prayer is an investment in eternity and true prayer is a romance of righteousness. Our fellowship is with the Father and with His Son Jesus Christ. Through prayer we participate in the communion of the God-kind; it's a throne-room caucus rendezvous: Jesus made it so! Oh, that the eyes of our understanding may be enlightened to see this awesome truth and that we may walk in the light of it! What a time of rich communion with the Lord prayer provides us!

Scripture enjoins us to pray without ceasing (1 Thessalonians 5:17). Prayer helps to season our spirits as a dependable receptacle for God's Spirit and power. Then we can connect to His ideas, visions and leadings more easily in order to change the world.

When we pray, we make tremendous power available, dynamic in its working, causing changes in our favour. Certain prayer sessions are specially designed by the Lord to help straighten out things in the spirit-realm regarding our immediate or later future as individuals, families or ministries. How wonderful that we can change circumstances and alter destinies in His Name through prayer! We serve a kind, loving, great and gracious God who daily loads us with benefits (Psalms 68:19). During times of prayer, we can meditate on His goodness and appropriate these benefits to our life's circumstances.

It is God's earnest desire to have a rich, vibrant and enduring fellowship with His children; but how can they enjoy such communion with Him if they don't know how to pray effectively? This is one of the many reasons He impressed it upon me to write *"HOW TO PRAY EFFECTIVELY"* and share with you some vital truths and principles of effective prayer. This first volume will help establish for you a clear understanding of the rules of different prayers for different situations and how to apply them for your desired outcome.

You can expect your prayer life to be revolutionized as you open your heart to receive and practice the divine insights that will be unveiled to you.

The Prayer of Faith

Chapter One

As believers in Christ, our life is a life of faith. "Faith" is one of the outstanding virtues that distinguish us from the unbeliever. For it's by faith that we accepted God's gracious salvation through Christ, thereby receiving eternal life (the God-kind of life) into our spirits. Our walk with God is a walk of faith. In Romans 1:16-17, Apostle Paul stated, *"For I am not ashamed of the gospel of Christ: for it is the power of God unto salvation to every one that believeth...For therein is the righteousness of God revealed from faith to faith: as it is written, The just shall live by faith."* This scripture thus confirms faith as a great underlying factor at the core of our existence as believers. *"But without faith it is impossible to please him..."* (Hebrews 11:6).

In our prayer life, the principle of faith holds sway in a significant context. The prayer of faith is one among the different kinds of prayer, and it has its peculiar rules and requirements. This prayer involves making a request to God and speaking to circumstances in order to make them conform to our desires, without doubts in our hearts.

In Mark 11:22, Jesus counselled His disciples to *"...HAVE FAITH IN GOD."* But it's interesting to know that the literal translation of His statement actually reads, "HAVE THE FAITH OF GOD." In other words, have the God-kind of faith.

When you understand this kind of faith the Lord Jesus was talking about and learn how to operate in it, you'll become well-equipped and ready to get results through your prayer of faith. I've taught extensively on the subject of different kinds of faith in another book: "How to Make Your Faith Work." But let's see what Jesus says here about having the faith of God.

In the subsequent verses following His profound statement, Jesus went on to tell us something so vital about the God-kind of faith.

"And Jesus answering saith unto them, Have faith in God. For verily I say unto you, That whosoever shall say unto this mountain, Be thou removed, and be thou cast into the sea; and shall not doubt in his heart, but shall 'believe' that those things which he saith shall come to pass; he shall have whatsoever he saith. Therefore I

say unto you, What things soever ye desire, when ye pray, 'believe' that ye receive them, and ye shall have them" (Mark 11:22-24).

The Master repeatedly uses the word "believe," emphasizing to us that "believing" is a fundamental requirement for having our desires met when we pray. Thus, one crucial question to ask at this point would be: What does it mean to believe?

You've got to understand that the Christian concept of "believing" is different from the unbeliever's idea of "believing." Anybody can believe a thing; the Bible says, *"Thou believest that there is one God; thou doest well: the devils also believe, and tremble. But wilt thou know, O vain man, that faith without works is dead?"* (James 2:19-20). You can see that even the demons "believe", but what distinguishes your "believing" as a child of God is your "works." And this is the type of "believing" Jesus was referring

to in Mark 11:23-24—the believing that acts
and takes possession.

> *"Therefore I say unto you, What
> things soever ye desire, when ye pray,
> 'believe' that ye receive them, and ye
> shall have them" (Mark 11:24).*

Notice Jesus didn't say, "When you pray, wait
until you get your request before you believe."
Rather, he told us to believe that we receive right
at the point of praying, and we would have our
request. This is faith! Faith means "I have it,
though I may not see it with my physical eyes
now." Therefore, "to believe" in the context of
Jesus' teaching in Mark 11:23-24 doesn't connote
an individual living in the realm of hope; rather,
it talks about a possessor—one who accepts that
something "exists," and thus "acts as such."

Principles Of The Prayer Of Faith

1) THERE MUST BE A SPECIFIC DESIRE

Specific desire is paramount in the prayer of faith. Jesus said: *"For verily I say unto you, That whosoever shall say unto this mountain, Be thou removed, and be thou cast into the sea; and shall not doubt in his heart, but shall believe that those things which he saith shall come to pass; he shall have whatsoever he saith"* (Mark 11:23).

Jesus emphasized the need for specificity of desire when we pray. Observe in the Scripture above that He didn't say, "Whosoever shall say to any mountain," but "Whosoever shall say to this mountain." Thus, in the prayer of faith, it's highly imperative that you have a clear and specific desire in your heart. You just can't be vague in your communication. You can act on God's Word in simplicity and faith and always expect results.

If you're a pastor, for example, and you wish to double the membership size of your church, you've got to know the exact number of people you have in church presently. So if you've got a fifty-member congregation at the moment, it means you're expecting to have a hundred members at a set time. This is what it means to be specific! Or perhaps, you want an increase in your finances. Then you should ask such questions like: What is my average annual income currently? How much more do I want to receive in the coming year?

Specificity is an essential principle if you must get effective results through the prayer of faith. Remember, Jesus said, *"whosoever shall say unto this mountain."* That means you're not going to be talking about the mountain, or telling God to do something about the mountain. You're to address the mountain and tell it what to do; the content of your prayer must be directed towards your specific area of need, otherwise you may not get the desired outcome.

2) SEE THE UNSEEN

Here is another vital principle to observe where the prayer of faith is concerned. You've got to see the unseen! You should be able to visualize what you desire, and it's only when your desire is specific that you can see it.

How do you see the unseen? Through the eyes of faith! Because you can't possess what you can't see.

> *"While we look not at the things which are seen, but at the things which are not seen: for the things which are seen are temporal; but the things which are not seen are eternal" (2 Corinthians 4:18).*

Abraham, the great patriarch of old, had to see the vision of God's promise to him to become a father of many nations. *"And he (God) brought him (Abraham) forth abroad, and said, Look now toward heaven, and tell the stars, if thou be able to number them: and he said unto him, So shall thy seed be. And he believed in the LORD; and he counted it to him for righteousness"* (Genesis 15:5-6).

As Joshua planned to attack Jericho, the Lord said to him, *"...See, I have given into thine hand Jericho, and the king thereof, and the mighty men of valour"* (Joshua 6:2). These two examples show us how imperative it is for us to have a mental picture of whatever our desire is. And here is the ultimate reason: The extent of your vision is the boundary of your blessing!

I love Dr. David Yongi Cho's testimony. He tells the story of how, many years ago, when he had just started out in the ministry and was pastoring a small church, he asked God to give him a chair, a table, and a bicycle. But God asked him what kind of chair, table, and bicycle he wanted, and he gave God his specifications.

Believing that he had received, he came before his congregation on Sunday morning and announced, "Praise God, I have a chair, a table, and a bicycle."

His members, young Christians who were just beginning to learn God's Word, asked incredulously, "But you walked to church today. Where's the bicycle?"

Of course, he had nothing to show his members, but he asserted that he had all the things he had mentioned. So after the service that day, some of his members decided to go home with him and find out if he really had those things.

On getting to his house and finding none of those items there, they asked him, "Where are the chair, table and bicycle."

"They're inside me," he answered. "I'm

pregnant with a chair, a table, and a bicycle!"

His members had to hold their stomachs for laughter, and they went around telling people, "Come see our pastor. He's pregnant with a chair, a table and a bicycle!" They had never heard anyone talk like that, but Pastor Cho had been able to see in reality the existence of those items. Through the eyes of faith, he had seen the unseen. And soon enough, the exact chair, table, and bicycle he had received by faith became a reality in the physical realm.

Understand this: "To see the unseen" isn't the same as "being optimistic." It actually means "to see the way God sees, and speak of the physically non-existent as though they already existed."

In his letter to the Roman Church, Paul shared something very instructive about the God-kind of faith:

"... even God, who quickeneth the dead, and calleth those things which be not as though they were" (Romans 4:17).

When you're so convinced that something is yours, even if you don't see it with your physical eyes, it's absolutely impossible for the devil or anyone to talk you out of it, because you've already possessed it by your faith, using the power of your thought.

3) USE YOUR EVIDENCE

According to Hebrews 11:1, faith is *"the substance of things hoped for, the evidence of things not seen."* The prayer of faith thus requires you to use the evidence you've got. But you must be able to recognize that evidence before you can use it.

You see, hope is a great virtue; it's a fundamental spiritual principle that arrays the magnificent future. But faith is the substance of things hoped for; it's the evidence that substantiates the future. If you had a piece of land, for instance, and you were told to prove your ownership of it, would you set out to move the property from its location to show anyone making an enquiry about the house? Of course, you wouldn't! In fact, you can't. What you'd simply do is to produce the title deed to the property.

In the Amplified Bible, faith is defined as *"...the assurance (the confirmation, THE TITLE DEED) of the things [we] hope for, being the proof of things [we] do not see {and} the conviction of their reality [faith perceiving as real fact what is not revealed to the senses]"* (Hebrews 11:1).

Now, when you seek to effect changes through the prayer of faith, you must be spiritually alert to recognize the evidence the Holy Spirit is bringing to your awareness. Sometimes, you'd have a note of victory in your inner-man through a word of prophecy. The word may not necessarily come from someone else; the Holy Spirit can simply put the utterance in your mouth as you pray, or bring a song to your spirit that causes great rejoicing within you. Never let go of such words, for they're the evidence of your victory. Meditate on them; talk them; be bold to let others know you've gotten it, and act the same way.

If perhaps you've been sick, and you've prayed to be healed, you need to look inside you for the evidence of your healing. Study the Word of God and find out what He has said about your peculiar situation today. When you've located the evidence, use it!

4) DON'T DOUBT AFTER YOU'VE PRAYED

When you've prayed for something you desire, it's important you don't allow doubt into your heart. This is a very essential rule that applies in the prayer of faith. Doubt makes us keep asking for the same thing over and over again for fear of not being heard the first time.

Unlike other kinds of prayer, such as the prayer of intercession or the prayer of petition, where repetitiveness is permissible, the rule of the prayer of faith says you should believe that you receive when you pray. Praying over and over for something implies that doubt has set in within your heart. For each time you repeat yourself, you invalidate your previous request. That's akin to a farmer who plants a seed one day and uproots it the next; then he plants it again and uproots the following day. That seed will never grow, and he'll never have a harvest from it no matter how much he desires a harvest. But your prayers don't have to be encumbered anymore; you don't have to struggle with doubts again.

Your spirit (which is "the real you") was programmed by God to respond to His Word.

The Bible says, *"For with the heart man believeth unto righteousness..."* (Romans 10:10). The "heart" here is the human spirit, which God seeks to influence. Thus, the Word of God in the human spirit establishes faith. But the human mind may raise doubtful questions as to the convictions of the human spirit. If this happens, it doesn't mean you've doubted in your heart. The doubting that opposes faith is that which may emanate from the human spirit. However, God's Word shows us how to deal with both kinds of doubt.

Dealing With Doubt In Your Mind

> *"For though we walk in the flesh, we do not war after the flesh: (For the weapons of our warfare are not carnal, but mighty through God to the pulling down of strongholds;) Casting down imaginations, and every high thing that exalteth itself against the*

knowledge of God, and bringing into captivity every thought to the obedience of Christ" (2 Corinthians 10:3-5).

"Strongholds" in this context connote arguments, theories or ideas that the society has sold to us. They form the basis for the "imaginations" of the ordinary man; his reasoning is molded by them. For example, a medical doctor has knowledge of facts and theories that form an integral part of his personality. Different people have their mentality shaped in one way or the other, by education, training or culture. And so, these diverse forms of knowledge tend to militate against the Word of God in their hearts, creating doubts in their minds. But the scripture in 2 Corinthians 10:3-5 lets us know they can be refuted using the weapons of our warfare: our divine utterances, speaking in other tongues, and our bold proclamation of the written Word of God. By these you'll pull down strongholds and cast down imaginations that arise from your mind.

Dealing With Doubt In Your Spirit

To doubt in your spirit means to be double-minded, or to waver or withdraw alternately from your conviction. James says, *"...he that wavereth is like a wave of the sea driven with the wind and tossed. For let not that man think that he shall receive any thing of the Lord. A double minded man is unstable in all his ways"* (James 1:6-8).

It also means to stagger at God's Word. The Bible says in Romans 4:20-21 that *"he (Abraham) staggered not at the promise of God through unbelief; but was strong in faith, giving glory to God; And being fully persuaded that, what he had promised, he was able also to perform"*

Abraham refused to stagger at the promise of God through unbelief; but was strong in faith. Strong faith is the antidote for doubt in your heart. When you find yourself staggering at God's Word and struggling to believe it; being double-minded and unstable; what you need to do is strengthen your faith. And this happens as you put your faith to work.

The more you put your faith to work, the stronger it becomes. If your faith is weak, it indicates there's doubt in your heart; and such weak faith is the result of not exercising your faith. The cure, therefore, for weak faith is acting on the Word, exercising your faith. If you want your faith to be strong, start doing the Word! For example, the Bible says, *"In every thing give thanks: for this is the will of God in Christ Jesus concerning you"* (1 Thessalonians 5:18). So what should you do? Start practising the scripture by giving God thanks. Let your life become an unending stream of praise and thanksgiving to God, irrespective of your situation or circumstances. That's acting on the Word!

5) WHAT YOU SAY IS WHAT YOU GET

Maintaining the right confession is another important prerequisite where the prayer of faith is concerned.

"Confession," in the New Testament portion of Scriptures, is derived from the Greek word "homologia," which literally means to speak the same thing in agreement with another. Thus, you agree with, and say what the Word of God says about you or your situation.

The Bible says that a man believes with his heart unto righteousness and confesses with his mouth unto salvation (Romans 10:10). That means until you confess that you're saved, you can't enjoy the benefits of salvation. You're made right with God when you believe, but it's your confession that brings you into the benefits of salvation—prosperity, divine health, preservation, favour, and so on.

As you make your demands through the prayer

of faith, never forget to employ the instrument of confession—constantly speaking in agreement with God's Word concerning the issue at hand. Words are powerful; they are the vehicles of your thoughts. They can affect your body, circumstances, and your entire life. What's more, your utterances as a child of God aren't mere words; they're inspired truths based on God's eternal Word.

Know Your Part and Do It

Chapter Two

f you didn't have the ability to believe God for something and have it come to pass, He wouldn't have told you to do so. God never tells you to do something you can't do.

When we make demands through the prayer of faith, it's so vital for us to know what role we're expected to play. Often, there's an act of obedience that God requires of us. Many people are ignorant of this truth, and so they fail to take the necessary steps besides praying. In the end, they would have reasons why their expectations weren't met. But when you're in sync with the Spirit of God in prayer, He'll show you what your role is, and you ought to be diligent to play your part.

When Christ ministered to certain people through the Word of faith, there was always something He required.

> *"And it came to pass, when Joshua was by Jericho, that he lifted up his eyes and looked, and, behold, there stood a man over against him with his sword drawn in his hand: and Joshua went unto him, and said unto him, Art thou for us, or for our adversaries? And he said, Nay; but as captain of the host of the LORD am I now come. And Joshua fell on his face to the earth, and did worship, and said unto him, what*

saith my lord unto his servant?"
(Joshua 5:13-14).

It was the Holy Spirit who referred to Himself here as the Captain of the Lord's Host. He came to tell Joshua what to do as he stood before Jericho, contemplating how best to take it. Jericho was a part of the Promised Land, and God said to Joshua, *"...see I have given into thine hand Jericho and the king thereof and the mighty men of valor"* (Joshua 6:2).

Notice He didn't say, "I will give...," but "I have given..." This wasn't a promise; it was a statement of fact coming from the mouth of God. It's quite remarkable that though God had given the Israelites Jericho, there were still great walls surrounding the city when they got there. The walls were so huge that the children of Israel couldn't scale over them. Even if they did, the armies of Jericho were in position to pick them off like sitting ducks. It seemed Israel would be unable to go in and possess the land the Lord had given to them. But the Holy Spirit, the Extraordinary Strategist, was present to tell Joshua what he needed to do to conquer Jericho:

> *"And ye shall compass the city, all ye men of war, and go round about the city once. Thus shalt thou do six days. And seven priests shall bear before the ark seven trumpets of rams' horns: and the seventh day ye shall compass the city seven times, and the priests shall blow with the trumpets. And it shall come to pass, that when they make a long blast with the ram's horn, and when ye hear the sound of the trumpet, all the people shall shout with a great shout; and the wall of the city shall fall down flat, and the people shall ascend up every man straight before him" (Joshua 6:3-5).*

The strategy given to Joshua was obviously strange (but supernatural), because no human mind would've thought of bringing down those walls through the mere sound of trumpets and the shout of weary men.

But the walls miraculously came down because Joshua and the host of Israel acted on the instruction of the Holy Spirit.

It's sad that many Christians have had promises from God that they never enjoyed, and prophecies that never came to pass, just because they didn't know what the Holy Ghost would have them do.

When the Lord told Joshua, "I've given you the city; I've given you the king and all the men of valor there. I've given all into your hand," Joshua could have shouted, "Wow, thank God, Jericho's mine!" and just gone to sleep. The next day he would have woken up to see those walls looming as defiantly as ever, and he would have wondered, *But God told me He had given the land into my hand; why can't He bring to pass what He promised?*

That's just like someone who says, "I thought God said the job was mine. I went there and they didn't give me the employment letter; in fact, they threw me out!"

Yours can be a different story. You can confidently declare God's Word in faith and get the results you want, as long as you're poised to follow the leading of the Spirit on that matter. To accomplish this, you need to fellowship with the Holy Spirit and find out the strategies to employ in order to have what you want.

Hearing From God

"The grace of our Lord Jesus Christ, and the love of God, and the COMMUNION of the Holy Ghost, be with you all. Amen" (2 Corinthians 13:14).

"Communion" refers to a partnership, a

communication, a fellowship with the Holy Spirit. It means talking to the Holy Spirit and listening to Him talk to you. This is how you get to know what He wants you to do. It's not enough to have a vision or to proclaim what you want; you've got to know the right steps to take to make that vision a reality, then you can go ahead and do it.

You see, it's not God's idea for us to always call on Him for our needs. Most of the time, our cries and pleas to God are unnecessary, for He's given us the power to bring about whatever kind of change we want in our lives.

Paul prayed in **Ephesians 1:17-18:**

> *"That the God of our Lord Jesus Christ, the Father of glory, may give unto you the spirit of wisdom and revelation in the knowledge of him: The eyes of your understanding being enlightened; that ye may know what is the hope of his*

*calling, and what the riches of the
glory of his inheritance in the saints."*

As you become acquainted with the great provisions that God has freely given you, not only would your prayer language change, you'd also begin to understand the necessary actions you need to take in order to enjoy your divine inheritance. You'd cease to pray the "Lord-give-me" prayers; instead, you'd be acting on the infallible Word of God and getting remarkable results. You'd know beyond doubt that all things are yours, and anything is indeed possible.

The Prayer of Petition

Chapter Three

In the literal sense, a petition is a formal written plea with legal demands. A petitioner writes according to legal guidelines and makes his request in such a way as to convince the one he is presenting his petition to. It is also defined as a solemn entreaty; a supplication or request appealing to an authority, or an earnest or humble appeal for something or to someone.

The prayer of petition does entail much seriousness; it's an earnest request accompanied with a great deal of intensity. However, its effectiveness or efficacy doesn't necessarily have to do with lengthiness. You can make far-reaching impact in your world and turn circumstances around in just a few minutes through the prayer of petition.

> *"I exhort therefore, that first of all, supplications, prayers, intercessions, and giving of thanks, be made for all men" (1Timothy 2:1).*

The word 'supplications' here also means 'petitions' or 'entreaties.' So, put differently, Apostle Paul was instructing Timothy to make petitions a priority in his prayers.

Praying According To The Will Of God

Another passage of Scripture that talks about 'petition' is **1 John 5:14–15:**

> *"And this is the confidence that we have in Him, that, if we ask anything according to his will, he heareth us: And if we know that he hear us, whatsoever we ask, we know that we have the petitions that we desired of him."*

Since praying according to the will of God is the key ingredient for success in the prayer of petition, it is important for us to understand exactly what it means to "ask according to God's will."

Many Christians have assumed, mostly as a result of their misconception of the Scriptures, that the reason they didn't receive answers to their prayers was because such prayers weren't in line with God's Will for them. They assume God didn't want them to have what they were asking for. But this is an erroneous interpretation of God's Word in the context of prayer. Let's look at the Scripture again:

> *"And this is the confidence that we have in him, that, if we ask any thing according to his will, he heareth us: And if we know that he hear us, whatsoever we ask, we know that we have the petitions that we desired of him" (1 John 5:14-15).*

Those who hold that mistaken notion that their prayers weren't answered because they didn't pray according to God's will fail to understand that the Holy Spirit's emphasis in this scripture isn't primarily the consistency of their request with God's will, but their exclusive privilege of having a hearing with God. Furthermore, when He tells us to *ask according to God's will,* He isn't talking about "WHAT" we ask for, but "HOW" we ask for it. In other words, the way and manner we present our petitions ought to be consistent with God's stipulated pattern. It's important to know, therefore, how to ask the Father according to His will for asking.

> *"And in that day ye shall ask me nothing. Verily, verily, I say unto you, Whatsoever ye shall ask the Father in my name, he will give it you. Hitherto have ye asked nothing in my name: ask, and ye shall receive, that your joy may be full...At that day ye shall ask in my name..." (John 16:23-24,26).*

Jesus, at this instance, introduced the exclusive deal—the new, acceptable way of asking from God. When you make requests to the Father in Jesus' Name, you're actually functioning in Jesus' stead. It's as though Jesus were the one making that request.

You know, some religious folks consider

praying directly to the Father a sacrilege; they'd rather resort to intermediaries such as Mary, or the Apostles, or some "saint." Some others think the best they can attain to is commune with Jesus, who will then intercede for them with God. But that's exactly what Jesus said He won't do: *"In that day you will ask in My name, and I do not say to you that I shall pray the Father for you; for the Father Himself loves you, because you have loved Me, and have believed that I came forth from God"* (John 16:26-27).

The Father doesn't need anyone to plead with Him before He does something for you or grants your request. He loves you unconditionally! And all He wants is for you to ask according to His will—in the Name of Jesus—and it's yours. His will for asking therefore is in the Name of Jesus.

(*For further teaching on praying in the Name of Jesus, get my book titled* **Praying The Right Way***.*)

Earnest, Heartfelt, Continued Prayer

"The earnest (heartfelt, continued) prayer of a righteous man makes tremendous power available [dynamic in its working]" (James 5:16b AMP).

The prayer of petition is earnest, heartfelt and continued. Some Christians don't understand earnestness in prayer, so they miss the benefits of its impact. To be earnest means to be intent and specific in purpose; to be zealous and fervent; marked by a deep feeling of conviction.

Thus, **an earnest prayer is specific in purpose, filled with zeal and fervency, and marked by a deep feeling of conviction.** It touches your heart and gets a hold of your emotions as you render it. Furthermore, it entails much persistence and continuance; that means you maintain your stance in a consistent manner and solemn attitude. This is the kind that makes tremendous power available; and such power is dynamic in its working; in other words, it works like dynamite.

Elijah's Prayer Of Petition

Elijah is an exemplary Bible character who made petitions to God in prayer and got results. And the Bible says that he *"...was a man subject to like passions as we are"* (James 5:17). He was like you and me, though not absolutely in the spiritual sense, because he didn't have the inherent divine nature we possess in Christ. But he was like us in the sense that the natural conditions of his time were very much like ours today. He faced the same kind of pressures we face today and had feelings, affections and a constitution as ours. Yet he prayed earnestly that it might not rain, and it didn't rain on earth for three-and-a-half years! He prayed again and the heavens gave rain and the earth brought forth her fruit.

"Elias was a man subject to like passions as we are, and he prayed earnestly that it might not rain: and it rained not on the earth by the space of three years and six months. And he prayed again, and the heaven gave rain, and the earth brought forth her fruit" (James 5:17-18).

When you read this story from the account in 1 Kings 17 alone, you may not get the exact picture of how events transpired. Here's what that passage says:

"... Elijah the Tishbite, who was of the inhabitants of Gilead said unto Ahab, As the Lord God of Israel liveth, before whom I stand, there shall not be dew nor rain these years but according to my word"(1 Kings 17:1).

This gives us the impression that Elijah just approached King Ahab one day and told him,

"There would be no dew or rain on the land for three-and-a-half years, but according to my word" and stormed out of his palace. It would seem that he spoke a word of faith and that was it. Well, it's true Elijah spoke in faith, but James' account in the New Testament shows us there was something behind the word of faith he spoke.

> *"Elias was a man subject to like passions as we are, and he prayed earnestly that it might not rain: and it rained not on the earth by the space of three years and six months"* (James 5:17).

Ever before Elijah went to Ahab to make his pronouncement, he had already spoken to God in his closet. This is something we must learn to do before making a public proclamation of our faith. If God is going to hear a man in public, He must have heard him first in private. Put differently, **before a public proclamation of**

faith, there must first be a private dealing with the Lord. This is so vital; but sadly, many Christians don't know it. Here, we see that Elijah made a bold declaration of faith that shook the king and the entire nation of Israel...but he had prayed earnestly.

In his account, James doesn't tell us about Elijah's public proclamation, but he does let us know he prayed earnestly that it shouldn't rain. God heard him and there was no rain for three-and-a-half years. Then he prayed earnestly again that the rains should fall, and God heard him and granted his request.

> *"And it came to pass after many days, that the word of the Lord came to Elijah in the third year, saying, Go, shew thyself unto Ahab; and I will send rain upon the earth"* **(1 Kings 18:1).**

Looking at this portion in isolation, one

could easily assume that Elijah was somewhere just having a nice time when God said, "Hey Elijah, I want to send rain! Go show yourself to Ahab and tell him it's going to rain."

But James makes us understand that Elijah had prayed that there should be rain. 1 Kings 18:1 was God's response to Elijah's prayer. Now, since God had already said, "I will send rain," you'd suppose that as soon as Elijah showed himself to Ahab, the rain would start falling. It didn't turn out that way!

Continue Until There's A Change

The Bible described Elijah's prayer as an earnest, heartfelt and **"continued"** prayer. There was persistence in his petition.

Many battles are lost because we stop too soon, instead of continuing in prayer. Many times we wait until pressures mount against us before we start praying. But at such times we end up pushing the panic-buttons; we start praying fast because we want fast answers. Since we live in an age where everything happens fast, we allow the jet-age syndrome sap the vitality that our prayers should convey. We have fast food, fast cars, fast airplanes, fast computers...everything moves fast, and we want God to move at our pace. We just want to push some buttons and expect a quick response; but it doesn't work that way.

Elijah knew better. He cast himself down upon the earth, put his head between his knees and prayed earnestly, with deeply involved emotions, continuing until there was a change (1 Kings 18:42). But unlike Elijah, some Christians today aren't willing to sacrifice the time and labour required in the prayer of petition.

If you're a student, you can't *continue* in prayer when the exam starts tomorrow morning. You knew the date for the exam; you had the time to pray and prepare. Now it's the night before, and you're suddenly awakened to prayer.

Think of a man whose wife has complications in labour. She's about to be taken into the intensive care unit. The man is frantically looking for prayer warriors now to join him in "emergency prayers." As she's being wheeled into the surgery room, the man is also running into God's emergency ward! He wants answers right now, but he had nine months to pray!

This is the problem with many in the Church today. It appears that the learning of faith has caused many to drift away from the essentials of effective prayer. So now they aren't as willing to linger in (tarry in) prayer as they should. But to live an all-round victorious life in Christ, you must become spiritually adroit in both areas. Plus your faith, you must have the willingness and tenacity to continue in prayer until you have a note of victory in your spirit.

When Is The Prayer Of Petition Required?

Petition prayer is required in situations beyond your personal control—circumstances dictated or influenced by forces beyond you.

For instance, you may not want it to rain on a certain day because you're planning an outdoor event on that day. You don't have absolute jurisdiction over the rain; a farmer in the same vicinity may want it to rain, and rightly so. Such a situation requires you to pray a prayer of petition. You've got to do more than just speak the word of faith. It requires *continued, earnest, and heartfelt prayer of petition.* If you had a trade dispute that ended up in court or problems with the government, or issues pitting you against powers beyond you, or you have found yourself in hollow circumstances, you require the prayer of petition. In other instances you desire something or a change outside your personal ability to control, you must pray the petition prayer.

The Prayer of Petition(2)

Chapter Four

*I*n **Isaiah 43:26** God said:

"Put me in remembrance: let us plead together: declare thou, that thou mayest be justified."

Did God make this statement because He's forgetful? Certainly not! This is an invitation for you to bring forth your arguments and strong reasons in pleading your case. You must be able to present the statements of fact, promises, and declarations He's made concerning the matter at hand.

In Hosea 14:2, the Bible also says, *"Take with you words, and turn to the Lord: say unto him, Take away all iniquity, and receive us graciously: so will we render the calves of our lips."* You see, God wants you to put Him in remembrance of His Word!

The portion of Scripture that follows below is a good example of a prayer of petition. After Peter and John had begun to work many miracles in the Name of Jesus, the authorities of their day were unable to deny the efficacy of their faith, but threatened and ordered them not to preach any further about Jesus. So they prayed.

> *"And when they heard that, they lifted up their voice to God with one accord, and said, Lord, thou art God, which hast made heaven, and earth, and the sea, and all that in them is: Who by*

the mouth of thy servant David hast said, Why did the heathen rage, and the people imagine vain things? The kings of the earth stood up and the rulers were gathered together against the Lord, and against his Christ. For of a truth against thy holy child Jesus, whom thou hast anointed, both Herod, and Pontius Pilate, with the Gentiles, and the people of Israel, were gathered together, For to do whatsoever thy hand and thy counsel determined before to be done. And now, Lord, behold their threatening: and grant unto thy servants, that with all boldness they may speak thy word, By stretching forth thine hand to heal; and that signs and wonders may be done by the name of thy holy child Jesus. And when they had prayed, the place was shaken where they were

assembled together; and they were all
filled with the Holy Ghost, and they
spake the word of God with boldness"
(Acts 4:24-31).

The content of this prayer is evidently based on God's Word. The apostles brought God's Word back to Him, putting Him in remembrance as they corporately pleaded their case. They spoke in specific terms based on His Word, and you should do likewise if you're making petitions in prayer.

Perhaps you want to see certain changes in your life, or in the life of a loved one; you must be sure to present your case to God with strong reasons, based on His Word. To pray like this is to stand on His sure Word that's immutable. In other words, when you're able to understand the mind of God on the subject of your prayer, such an understanding becomes the confidence and authority upon which your petitions are made. Hannah, the mother of prophet Samuel, prayed this way to get her miracle.

Hannah Brought Forth Her Strong Reasons

Hannah had been married to Elkanah for years, but she bore him no child. In contrast, Elkanah's other wife, Peninnah, had several children and would often taunt Hannah because of her barrenness. This caused her to be sad, and she cried for a child all the time. But one day she got tired of crying and made up her mind to have a change.

So she went into the house of the Lord, fell on her face before God and brought forth her case. Her words were barely heard because she prayed silently to God. The serving high priest even misjudged her, thinking she was drunk. *"How long will you make a drunken spectacle of yourself?" He rebuked her. "Put away your wine"* (1 Samuel 1:14 NRSV). But Hannah answered,

"No, my lord, I am a woman deeply troubled; I have drunk neither wine nor strong drink, but I have been pouring out my soul before the LORD. Do not regard your servant as a worthless woman, for I have been speaking out of my great anxiety and vexation all this time" (1Samuel 1:15-16 NRSV).

Many have thought that Hannah simply made a vow to God, but she did more. She actually made a petition to God, giving Him strong reasons why she should have a child. And her prayer was answered.

> *"Then Eli answered, "Go in peace; the God of Israel grant the petition you have made to him." And she said, "Let your servant find favor in your sight." Then the woman went to her quarters, ate and drank with her husband, and her countenance was sad no longer...Elkanah knew his wife Hannah, and the LORD remembered*

her. In due time Hannah conceived and bore a son. She named him Samuel, for she said, "I have asked him of the LORD" (1 Samuel 1:17-20 NRSV).

When you pray the prayer of petition, always make certain that you present your case in a compelling way, such that it can't be denied. And refuse to quit until you get that note of victory.

Turn Your Closet Into A Courtroom!

The prayer of petition is rendered with tenacity and strong purpose. You don't take "no" for an answer! If you don't get a note of victory the first time you pray, it only means "Case Adjourned!" You can go back again to pray about it, just like a plaintiff goes to a higher court to appeal an unsatisfactory decision. Your prayer closet becomes a courtroom where you plead your case. And when you know you've gotten what you wanted, nothing in the world can take it from you.

Don't Stop At The Prophecy!

"And Elijah said unto Ahab get thee up eat and drink for there is a sound of abundance of rain" (1Kings 18:41).

I've seen people who received anointed words just like this one but didn't do what Elijah did. And when the prophecy they got didn't come to pass, they wondered what had happened. Well, it didn't come because they didn't follow it up!

Notice that Elijah didn't stop at prophesying an abundance of rain; he did something more. He prayed!

When King Ahab went up to eat and drink, Elijah didn't join him to feast. Instead, he went to the top of Mount Carmel to pray. Though the prophetic word he'd received assured him there'd be abundant rain, Elijah still went to pray. Remember, it wasn't God who shut the heavens, so He wasn't obliged to determine when to open it up. It was Elijah who prayed to shut the heavens, and now he had to pray with just as much intensity for the heavens to be opened.

Many Christians often make the mistake of stopping at the prophecy instead of using the prophetic word to continue in prayer. Too many times, people have their desire just within reach and somehow still don't get it. This is the reason someone may have the contract he bid for approved, without ever getting the approval letter. Then he begins to wonder what in the world happened. Yes, he heard the sound of the abundance of rain all right, but he didn't follow-up with the right kind of prayer. This is where many stop and their dreams become stillborn.

The Prayer Of Petition Brings Forth A Strong Anointing

"And said to his servant, Go up now, look toward the sea. And he went up, and looked, and said, There is nothing. And he said, Go again seven times" (1 Kings 18:43).

Seven times, Elijah sent his servant out to go check the clouds. You must however understand that this wasn't done in quick succession. Each time the servant returned, he found Elijah still praying intensely, and all he did was look up and say to the servant, "Go and check again." This happened seven times and could have been over several hours, if not days.

"And it came to pass at the seventh time, that he said, behold there ariseth a little cloud out of the sea like a man's hand. And he said, Go up, say unto Ahab, prepare thy chariot, and

get thee down, that the rain stop thee not'. And it came to pass in the mean while, that the heaven was black with clouds and wind, and there was a great rain. And Ahab rode, and went to Jezreel. And the hand of the Lord was on Elijah; and he girded up his loins, and ran before Ahab to the entrance of Jezreel" (1 Kings 18: 44-46).

Elijah outran King Ahab's chariot which must've been the finest and fastest in the land. He could do so because the hand of the Lord was upon him. When you pray like he prayed, the anointing of God's Spirit comes upon you strongly, and you can do or change anything, Hallelujah!

God gave us power in the Holy Ghost to effect changes, and we have unlimited influence through the prayer of petition. Through this kind of prayer, a man can reverse a death sentence passed on him either by state laws for a crime he committed, or by an incurable disease. You can even bring a loved-one out of prison with this kind of prayer. Yes, you can cancel any undesirable verdict written against you. There's nothing you can't do or change when you pray the earnest, heartfelt, continued prayer of the righteous. As you present every matter of concern before the Lord, giving Him your strong reasons as backed by the Word, you'll be incubating upon that matter, and there'll surely be changes in your favour.

Praying With The Spirit

Chapter Five

*P*raying with the spirit means to pray in other tongues, and it's a very important kind of prayer for the believer. Some people have questions about it, but that's because they don't understand what it's all about. "Is it really compulsory we pray in other tongues?" they ask. "Does every Christian have to pray in tongues?" Usually, questions and arguments about praying in tongues come from those who don't pray in tongues. You'd rarely find a Christian who prays in tongues questioning this manifestation of the spirit. In Mark 16:17, the Lord Jesus said, *"And these signs shall follow them that believe; In my name shall they cast out devils; they shall speak with new tongues..."*

"Them that believe" refers to Christians, those who have been born again. So if you're a believer in Christ, you should speak in tongues.

Many of those who argue against speaking and praying in tongues don't know why it's so important. They're unaware of the bountiful benefits that this spiritual exercise brings. Let us now explore some of the glorious benefits of praying in tongues.

Praying In Tongues Refreshes And Revives

"For with stammering lips and another tongue will he speak to this people. To whom he said, This is the rest wherewith ye may cause the

weary to rest; and this is the refreshing: yet they would not hear" (Isaiah 28:11-12).

This prophecy from Isaiah relates to speaking in tongues, and it helps us to understand one of the reasons we should pray in tongues. Paul, also accentuating the same thing, stated that *"He that speaketh in an unknown tongue edifieth himself...."* (1 Corinthians 14:4) In other words, he charges up, builds up, overhauls, or refreshes himself. Praying in tongues refreshes and revives you.

A Christian may suddenly realize he doesn't preach the gospel as much anymore because he's not as excited, inspired or motivated as he was when he just gave his heart to Christ. This ought not to be. You should always be motivated and excited about the things of the Spirit; and the way to continually fuel this inspiration of the Holy Spirit and keep the fire of soul-winning burning in your heart is by praying in other tongues. When you pray fervidly in tongues, the fire in your spirit burns to God's glory.

Getting yourself stirred up in the things of God isn't and shouldn't be a mystery. He's already shown the "how" to you through His Word. So it's no use praying, "Revive me, O Lord!" You're revived when you speak in tongues. This is the secret. So take out time on your own and speak in other tongues. When you do, you'll be edifying, refreshing and beautifying your spirit.

Praying In Tongues Brings Forth The Leading of The Spirit

It is important for Christians to spend time praying with or in the spirit—that is, praying in tongues. The Bible says, *"For as many as are led by the Spirit of God, they are the sons of God"* (Romans 8:14). The leading of the Spirit is not an experience meant for apostles, prophets, evangelists, pastors and teachers only, but also for every child of God. We all ought to live our lives perpetually by the leading of the Spirit. God's children should never be in the dark or get into unpleasantly surprising situations where they wouldn't know what to do. When we pray in tongues, it's an opportune moment for us to receive the divine guidance and direction of the Holy Spirit for our lives.

> *"Howbeit when he, the Spirit of truth, is come, he will guide you into all truth: for he shall not speak of himself; but whatsoever he shall hear, that shall he speak: and he will shew you things to come" (John 16:13).*

When you pray in other tongues, your spiritual eyes are opened to understand the Scriptures in a greater light. This is my daily experience. Sometimes, people ask me how I got the interpretation to certain Scriptures they had read but didn't clearly understand. Always, I'd reply that it's by the Spirit. When you spend time to pray in other tongues, the eyes of your understanding are enlightened and you become more receptive to the ministry of the Holy Spirit.

Praying In Tongues Provides Us With Heaven's Vocabulary

One of the most beautiful and inspiring gifts from God to us is the ability to communicate with Him directly through a spiritual language formed in us by the Holy Spirit. We speak divine mysteries and alter destinies through this supernatural effusion.

Remember that though man is a spirit, he doesn't dwell 'physically' in the realm of the spirit. He lives on earth and relates with the material world. Yet there're certain things we can't communicate or express with the earthly languages we've learnt. This is the reason God imparts to us the divine ability to speak in other tongues, so we can have the right language (vocabulary) to communicate with God. If you have a little child that hasn't started talking fluently, you can't have fellowship with that child. You may play with him and enjoy games with him, but you can't have *real* fellowship with him because real fellowship requires a two-way communication.

> *"...he that speaketh in an unknown tongue speaketh not unto men, but unto God: for no man understandeth him..." (1 Corinthians 14:2).*

When you speak in other tongues, no one understands what you're saying, because you're speaking to God. It's a direct communication between your spirit and God. You're speaking the language that only He understands.

You must realize that there are not enough words in human vocabulary to adequately and accurately express ourselves to God. It doesn't matter how many earthly languages you can speak, you still won't have enough vocabulary to express yourself to Him, because in the realm of the spirit, there are things we can't communicate with all of the languages of the world. This is why it is absolutely necessary for a Christian to speak and pray in tongues.

In addition, when we speak to God with human words, we may sometimes speak words that are unacceptable to Him, but the Holy Ghost, knowing this, gives us a language with which to express ourselves. When we speak in this language, everything we say is articulately communicated to God and there's a two-way communication—we speak to God and He speaks back to us through our spirits.

This is why a Christian must be filled with the Holy Ghost. He's the One Who gives us the utterance to speak in this language by which we can communicate with the Father articulately, beyond earthly expressions. It's a holy, heavenly language.

Praying In Tongues Helps Reveal The Will Of God

Many people wonder if it's possible to know the will of God. Some Christians even quote a line from a popular song by William Cowper, saying, "God moves in mysterious ways, His wonders to perform." Obviously, they're quoting the song out of context, because God surely isn't mysterious and doesn't work in mysterious ways. He's revealed Himself and His Will to us primarily through His written Word. But we can also know God's Will when we pray in other tongues. The Holy Spirit will never lead you outside the provisions of God's Word. When you pray with the spirit, the Holy Spirit imparts to you the knowledge of God's will concerning issues of importance. Remember, Jesus said, *"...when he, the Spirit of truth, is come, he will guide you into all truth: for he shall not speak of himself; but whatsoever he shall hear, that shall he speak: and he will shew you things to come"*

(John 16:13).

When you pray in the spirit, your mind doesn't grasp the meaning of the utterances you make, but the Holy Spirit is able to bring the interpretation to your understanding.

When I pray sometimes, I speak some words in other tongues as a sort of reply to what I've been praying about. A lot of times, such words are given by the Holy Spirit as answers to questions, as solutions to problems. They represent the wisdom you need to deal with pressing situations. And it's important you don't allow such words go without putting them to good use. This is why the Bible instructs that when you pray in an unknown tongue, you ought to ask God for its interpretation, for often, in it lies the answer to your petition.

> *"Wherefore let him that speaketh in
> an unknown tongue pray that he may
> interpret. For if I pray in an unknown*

tongue, my spirit prayeth, but my understanding is unfruitful. What is it then? I will pray with the spirit, and I will pray with the understanding also: I will sing with the spirit, and I will sing with the understanding also" **(1 Corinthians 14:13-15).**

When the interpretation comes to your spirit, that's when you learn certain secrets. The Bible says the secret of God is with them that fear Him (Psalm 25:14). When you receive the interpretation, you'll find yourself being brought close to the deep realities of God. You're let into a body of wisdom reserved for the spiritual. Sometimes, you may begin to get these revelations in part, but you'd definitely have an idea of what God wants you to do.

You see, praying in tongues helps us to know and establish God's will for our lives; it enables us to shape the circumstances of our environment to be in conformity with His plans and purposes.

Praying In Tongues Helps You Bring Forth God-Ideas

Often, there're certain changes you want to see in your life, family, ministry, job, business, finances or academics, but they seem not to be happening. If you would pray in the spirit well enough, you would receive ideas and answers from the Holy Spirit through your spirit. And even when those ideas come to you in other tongues, the same Spirit of God can help you understand and put them to work.

When you find yourself at the crossroads of a major decision, you don't have to go about asking others what to do. You might get yourself confused that way, because you might be talking to the wrong people.

Some people think they'd have to wait a long time for an answer as men did in the Old

Testament. But we live in a new age today! In this dispensation, the One who answers you lives inside you. As you pray in other tongues, you'll speak forth answers to the issues at hand.

This was how I got God's direction for the very first crusade I organized. I had known about interpretation of tongues, but hadn't experienced it. I had been praying about the crusade and began speaking in tongues. I knew the Lord had a message which I was bringing forth in tongues. So I declared, "Lord Jesus, I know you're talking to me about something and it's coming in other tongues. But there's no one here to interpret the message. Therefore, Lord, I receive the gift of interpretation of tongues now, because I've got to know what you're telling me."

Suddenly, the anointing came on me and I began to interpret in English what the Spirit was saying. Then I recognized that the Lord was instructing me on certain things I needed to do for the crusade. Quickly, I wrote those things down and went and did as instructed, and we had an outstanding meeting. This spiritual exercise has since been a part of my daily Christian living, and I've experienced tremendous blessings practising it.

The Spirit of God does talk to you and always seeks to bring you divine ideas; one of the ways to hear Him and take a hold of His wisdom and extraordinary strategies is by praying in other tongues.

Get In The Flow And Maintain The Glow

In Acts 1:8 Jesus said, *"But ye shall receive power after that the Holy Ghost is come upon you."* The Greek word translated power here is "dunamis," which refers to a kind of power that's able to reproduce itself. The "dynamo," an electric power generating mechanical device, was named from this word. Now, another important benefit of praying in other tongues is that it gets you filled with the Holy Spirit and helps you maintain your spiritual glow.

Back in the Old Testament, they always needed a revival. David asked in Psalm 85:6, *"Wilt thou not revive us again: that thy people may rejoice in thee?"* But as born-again Christians, we don't have to ask for a revival, because we simply don't need it. In fact, if you check through the Scriptures, you'll discover that none of the apostles ever asked for a revival; they'd received a unique blessing that the Old Testament folks didn't have—the grace to be indwelt by the Holy Spirit, and the ability to stir up His divine power within themselves.

"And suddenly there came a sound from heaven as of a rushing mighty wind, and it filled all the house where they were sitting. And there appeared unto them cloven tongues like as of

fire, and it sat upon each of them. And they were all filled with the Holy Ghost, and began to speak with other tongues, as the Spirit gave them utterance" (Acts 2:2-4).

As a believer, you can constantly have the same experience the early apostles had. As you pray in other tongues, the same glory comes upon you, and you can maintain it twenty-four hours of the day, seven days of the week, and three hundred and sixty-five days of the year. Your prayer life becomes an exciting, everyday relationship with God.

Sometimes, I hear certain people say, "I don't know how to evangelize. I don't know how to start up a conversation about Jesus." What they need to do is to spend some time to pray in other tongues. When this is done before setting out, they'd be emboldened to preach the gospel with gusto.

The Bible records about the early Church in Acts 4:31 that *"...when they had prayed, the place was shaken where they were assembled together; and they were all filled with the Holy Ghost, and they spake the word of God with boldness."*

Some have the wrong idea about being drunk in the spirit. They think it's all about staggering around and scattering things. But thank God you've learnt the right thing to do with the influence of the Holy Spirit. You ought to speak forth the wisdom of God and make declarations of His divine mysteries. At such times, the gifts of the Spirit are manifested and miracles take place.

In the face of daunting opposition, what you need do is get in the flow of God's Spirit and maintain the glow by speaking in other tongues. As soon as you do that, that cloak of heaviness will be lifted from you and the joy of the Spirit will flood your heart. This is what brings the desired change.

This was what brought Paul the visions he got in his day. It sustained John on the Island of Patmos even when there was nobody to fellowship with him. In Revelation 1:10 He tells us, *"I was in the Spirit on the Lord's day, and heard behind me a great voice, as of a trumpet."*

Speaking in other tongues brings you in synchrony with the Holy Spirit so you can receive guidance and directions in God's will for your life.

The Prayer of Agreement

Chapter Six

*G*od has given us several means for effecting changes in the earth, and one of these is the prayer of agreement.

In Matthew 18:19 Jesus said, *"...if two of you shall agree on earth as touching any thing that they shall ask, it shall be done for them of my Father which is in heaven"*

These are the words of the Master Himself,

so they must be true.

> *"And I will give unto thee the keys of the kingdom of heaven: and whatsoever thou shalt bind on earth shall be bound in heaven: and whatsoever thou shalt loose on earth shall be loosed in heaven"* (Matthew 16:19).

The word "key" in Scripture speaks of authority, laws and principles. Here, Jesus didn't mean to say when you bind the devil on earth, he's also being bound in heaven. No, the devil doesn't operate in heaven, so God doesn't have to bind him there! When you "bind" something on earth, it simply means that your decree is backed up by God in heaven because there's provision for it in His Word. The Good News Bible (Today's English Version) puts it this way: "...*what you prohibit on earth will be prohibited in heaven, and what you permit on earth will be permitted in heaven.*" Glory to God!

Requirements For The Prayer Of Agreement

"Again I say unto you, That if two of you shall agree on earth as touching any thing that they shall ask, it shall be done for them of my Father which is in heaven" (Matthew 18:19).

In this statement made by Jesus, you find the requirements for a prayer of agreement:

1. The participants must be on earth

2. There must be at least two of them

3. They must agree

4. They must ask or make the definite request

Many Christians have yet to operate in this power because they're mostly inclined to begging God in their prayers. The reason we can (and should) issue commands and make decrees is because God assured us in His Word that our demands will be backed up by heaven. Remember, the Bible says, *"God is not a man, that he should lie; neither the son of man, that he should repent: hath he said, and shall he not do it? or hath he spoken, and shall he not make it good?"* (Numbers 23:19). He doesn't go back on His Word; He's got enough power to back it up with action.

There's a remarkable record in the Bible of how the prayer of agreement works. Herod, in his persecution of the Church, had killed James. When he observed that this pleased the people, he proceeded to arrest Peter, with full intentions of doing to him what he had done to James. But with the death of James, the Church had learnt their lesson and weren't going to allow the same fate befall Peter.

"And when he had apprehended him, he put him in prison, and delivered him to four quaternions of soldiers to keep him; intending after Easter to bring

him forth to the people. Peter therefore was kept in prison: but prayer was made without ceasing of the church unto God for him" (Acts 12:4-5).

Members of the early church must have decreed God's Word concerning Peter's situation. I can imagine that at their meetings, they joined their hands together and made special decrees in the Name of Jesus concerning his release. They couldn't have been crying, "O God, please have mercy on Peter; please deliver him!" If that was what they did, we wouldn't have this glorious testimony that has inspired generations of the Church!

They didn't ask God to do anything because Jesus had already taught them how to pray; He'd taught them not to make vain repetitions like the heathens who think they'd be heard for their much speaking. Thus, these believers simply made bold declarations in the Name of Jesus and their words were established.

This is how we ought to pray. I would to God that Christians prayed more of such prayers when visiting with one another. Some believers come together and all they talk about is how bad things have gone and how much evil is happening in the world. If only we would learn to join our hands together and call for changes in the Name of Jesus, our world would be a lot better! That's what Christians are supposed to do!

In the case of Peter, he'd been put in jail, bound with chains and guarded by soldiers, with a death sentence hanging over his head. But the Church couldn't sleep; they got together and held a prayer vigil for Peter's release while he slept! Even when some of those who prayed for Peter doubted, God still answered. That's because in the prayer of agreement, doubting by one or some of the parties involved doesn't nullify the agreement. We'll see this when we read some more of that story in Acts 12.

"And as Peter knocked at the door of the gate, a damsel came to hearken, named Rhoda. And when she knew Peter's voice, she opened not the gate for gladness, but ran in, and told how Peter stood before the gate. And they said unto her, Thou art mad. But she constantly affirmed that it was even so. Then said they, It is his angel. But Peter continued knocking: and when they had opened the door, and saw him, they were astonished" (Acts 12:13-16).

The prayers for Peter's deliverance had been answered; God had sent His angel to set him loose from Herod's maximum security prison (Acts 12:7-12). So When Rhoda got to the door and heard Peter's voice, she forgot to open the door and ran back in excitement to give others the good news.

"Brethren, the prayer meeting is over. It's

time for a praise meeting," she announced. "Apostle Peter is at the door!"

Some immediately said she had gone mad. Others concluded Herod had killed Peter and she must have seen his ghost. When they eventually mustered enough courage to open the door due to Peter's persistent knocking, the Bible says, "they were astonished." But these were the same folks who had just been praying and asking for Peter's release. There he was, standing at the door, and they were wondering if it was really him or his angel!

What matters is the agreement we have regarding what we ask. Remember, the prayer of faith requires that you don't doubt in your heart at all, but the prayer of agreement doesn't give that stringent condition. The fundamental requirement is the agreement between the participants at the time of prayer. Even if doubts come up in anyone's heart later on, your request isn't nullified because it wasn't made in doubt.

Thus, it can't be cancelled simply because one party doubted. For the request to be nullified, all the parties would've to come together again to cancel it.

Many times when people agree in prayer they aren't aware of these rules; so when one party doubts, he thinks he has cancelled the agreement. But it's not true. If it took two of you to agree, it would take both of you to cancel it! Otherwise, it can't be cancelled.

A Prayer Of Agreement Is A Decree

The principle of agreement doesn't refer only to two or more Christians coming together to make requests for the supply of a need. It's a kind of prayer that carries with it a decree and spells out certain things that must be established, as we find in the book of Job: *"Thou shalt also decree a thing, and it shall be established unto thee...*" (Job 22:28).

A prayer of agreement has to do with establishing a decree authoritatively—not begging that something be done. This is how the Church, based on Scripture, carries on the work of the gospel. This is how we execute the will of God in the earth. We come together and agree and decree how things should be, based on our knowledge of the Father's will.

For example, when people are ordained into the ministry and hands are laid on them, it's not just for the sake of blessing them; rather, such a consecration helps pave the way for great works to be done in and through their lives, and God, on His part, establishes those things based on the agreement.

The Church has so much power that many of God's people don't know about yet. This is why some Christians still act like ordinary people who have no power. The reality, however, is that you have a supernatural kind of power, more than enough to accomplish whatever you want. What you need is the knowledge of the Word, and the boldness of the Spirit.

There's Nothing We Can't Do When We Agree!

"Again I say unto you, That if two of you shall agree on earth as touching any thing that they shall ask, it shall be done for them of my Father which is in heaven" (Matthew 18:19).

Jesus said that if any two of us shall agree on earth as touching anything, it shall be done for us by the Father. Think about that word "ANYTHING"; it implies "no limits." Praise God!

The Church is the Body of Christ; we represent Him and carry on His work on earth today. We are His ambassadors.

Jesus stated that all things are possible to

those who believe, and you're one of them. Therefore, with the prayer of agreement, you can do anything; you can have miracles take place in the Name of Jesus Christ.

I was in my office one Sunday evening when a member of our church came in to see me, looking very sad. I asked her to sit down and tell me what the problem was, and she told me how she had applied for a visa and found it difficult to get one. The embassy had issued a visa to her sister but turned down her own request. As she narrated her ordeal, she started crying, but I began to laugh.

Then I said to her, "Do you remember that Jesus said if two of us shall agree on earth concerning anything we shall ask, it shall be done for us?"

I let her know we couldn't be stopped when we agree, and we could get whatever we wanted.

I prayed a simple prayer of agreement with

her, saying, *"Father, thank you in the Name of the Lord Jesus Christ because she's got her visa. No one can stop her."*

I told her to go back there and she would get her visa. When she went back to the embassy, she was given the visa as we had agreed in prayer. That's the power of the prayer of agreement!

The Prayer of Intercession

Chapter Seven

The Holy Spirit has an intercessory ministry which He carries out through believers. But there's also the intercessory ministry of the believer, which is quite different from the former.

The Holy Spirit does carry out His intercessory ministry through you. The Lord may tell you to pray for someone or minister to someone by the leading of His Spirit.

Sometimes, you may just be praying about personal issues and the Spirit of God suddenly begins to work within you, prompting you to intercede for an individual you never even planned to pray for.

However, you don't always have to wait for that prompting before you pray for others. As a child of God, you have a responsibility to intercede for others. You can decide by yourself to pray for someone without the Holy Spirit necessarily prodding you to do so. When you intercede for others this way and in accordance with the Word, it will be heard by God in just the same way as though the Holy Spirit inspired the words you spoke. It would just be as though the Holy Spirit Himself carried out that particular ministry.

Through the prayer of intercession, God bestows on us opportunity, ability and inspiration to make great impacts in our world. He has set us on the earth in these extraordinary times for the purpose of changing lives.

> *"...if thou altogether holdest thy peace at this time, then shall there enlargement and deliverance arise...*
>
> *from another place;...and who knoweth whether thou art come to the kingdom for such a time as this?" (Esther 4:14).*

Recognize that it's your priestly responsibility to intercede for others, and it's always a blessing to function in that office. Through prayer, we hold sway over satanic forces that seek to influence governments and nations for evil. Circumstances move in favour of God's plans and purposes for His people as they did for Deborah and Barak of old: they fought from heaven; the stars in their courses fought on their behalf against their adversaries.

Rules For Intercessory Prayer

1.   You don't intercede for yourself, because intercession is always for others.

2.   You can continue to pray about the same thing over and over again until the change comes.

In the prayer of intercession, your objective is to prevail on someone else to align with God's will. You're concentrating the influence of God's power towards others for their good, and that requires some persistence in prayer. That means you must be willing to continue in prayer for as long as is required until you get that note of victory in your spirit and are certain that you have what you asked for, you don't stop praying.

Intercessions—A Divine Responsibility

You have a personal ministry as a child of God to intercede for others. So many things can be changed if only you'd pray about them. There are three important points I want you to note about prayer, especially as it relates to intercessions:

1.   Prayer is a privilege; it's a great way of maintaining a relationship with the Lord.

2.   Prayer is also a command and a divine responsibility given us by God.

Paul expressed this in his letter to Timothy, *"I exhort therefore, that, first of all, supplications, prayers, intercessions, and giving of thanks, be made for all men"* (1 Timothy 2:1).

3.   Prayer is a discipline.

This is why you must pray even when you don't feel like it.

The prayer of intercession isn't meant for unbelievers only, but also for fellow believers. This much Samuel communicated to the Israelites when he said, *"Moreover as for me, God forbid that I should sin against the LORD in ceasing to pray for you: but I will teach you the good and the right way:"* (1 Samuel 12:23).

John also admonishes us to do the same: *"If any man see his brother sin a sin which is not unto death, he shall ask, and he shall give him life for them that sin not unto death..."* (1 John 5:16).

Labouring In Prayer

"Epaphras, who is one of you, a servant of Christ, saluteth you, always laboring fervently for you in prayers, that ye may stand perfect and complete in all the will of God" (*Colossians* 4:12).

Epaphras laboured fervently in prayer for the Colossian Christians. This is intercession, and it doesn't suggest an easy prayer with casual expressions like, "Father, I pray for Johnny. Bless him and answer his prayers; give him whatever he wants from You."

Paul, by the unction of the Spirit, talked about agonizing in prayer. It's a struggle that's similar to fighting, but not a fight with demons. It's a fight against the dictates of your flesh. Hence, Paul lets us know there's labour in this kind of prayer. It may not be enjoyable, but you discipline yourself to do it.

Some people think they ought to pray only when they're in the mood to pray, or when they feel the Holy Spirit is prompting them to do so. But the same persons go to work every day of the week even when they sometimes don't feel like going. They've simply disciplined themselves to do what's right as far as their job is concerned.

This is what prayer—especially intercessory prayer—should be for the Christian. It's your life's work, and you must do it even when it's not exciting. Since you've got a goal and want to prevail on circumstances to change, you must maintain discipline in prayer. At the beginning, it may not be very interesting, but you have to put all you've got into it. Stir up yourself and respond to God from your spirit. When you do this consistently, it'll become a part of you.

Don't Become Callous!

You may have used the Word of God successfully in many areas of your life, but there're people who are yet to walk in the reality of God's blessing and God wants you to be of help to them. This is why you need to intercede. There're many people who are hurting and if you can't be touched by their suffering, you can't be moved to pray for them.

Some Christians have become quite callous. The sinner's condition doesn't move them; the plights of the poor, the sick and the downtrodden don't touch them. They say, *"Well, it's because they wouldn't receive God's Word.*" They've become so cold-hearted that it's rare for the Holy Spirit to move them to pray for such people. Yet the Bible says of the Lord Jesus that He was touched with the feeling of our infirmities (Hebrews 4:15).

Prayer, sometimes, is the response to the impression of the Spirit in our hearts, or the impression the circumstances of others makes on our hearts, which compels us to want to cause a change.

I remember the testimony of a young girl who had been retarded and imprisoned by juvenile arthritis. She could only move in a wheelchair and was kept in bed most of the time. The only thing she could move freely was her neck, as this evil disease had stiffened her body. She was taken to a healing service, and while in that meeting she wept and called on the Lord to heal her.

Some others saw her and began to pray for her too. As they interceded for her, she told the lady beside her she wanted to get up. Though her hands and legs felt very heavy and painful, she managed to stand up with help from those around her. They encouraged her to move her arms and legs, and, inspired by their faith, she took her first few gingerly steps. The congregation was very excited and they kept on praying for her and encouraging her. Her faith was strengthened, and she took firmer steps. Before long, she was running around the room

Those people weren't moved by pity but by the compassion of Jesus, and they interceded for her. There's so much we can do and change if we'd learn to intercede for others.

Develop The Intercessor In You

You can train yourself to become an effective intercessor, and to do that, you're going to train yourself to spend time in prayer.

As a student in high school, I couldn't run very fast. Since sprinting was out of the question for me, I began to think of something else I could participate in during our annual sports day. Then I figured that since there were people who could run very fast but not for long, there'd also be those who might not be able to run very fast but could run for a long period.

I concluded that I fell in that second category and started training for long-distance running with a friend. We chose to try the 800m race, and very early every morning, we did several laps around the school field.

Though I eventually didn't run in any competitive race, I practised. It was tough going at first, and I felt like quitting after the first lap, but I discovered it got easier each morning we trained. After some weeks of consistent practice, not only was I able to complete the laps, I was also able to maintain my speed and even go faster.

I learnt a powerful principle from this: anything you practise consistently long enough will get into your system and become a part of you.

I also discovered I could break myself spiritually and discipline myself to pray using this principle. I would set the alarm on my clock to wake me up at a certain time during the night, and then I'd spend some time praying for different people and events. The more I did this, the easier it became, until I didn't need an alarm clock to wake me up anymore. It just became natural for me to get up at that time to pray. At the beginning it was hard, but I knew I didn't need anybody to do it for me; it was my responsibility to train myself to pray. This is what you must do also.

Remember, the rule in intercession is that you're persistent and continue in prayer for as long as is necessary. You don't stop praying until you have a note of victory in your spirit. When you do, you'll find yourself singing or laughing in the spirit. This laughter comes from your spirit. As David said, your heart begins to "indite" a good matter (Psalm 45:1). You bubble over with joy and laughter from your spirit. That's when you know your ministry of intercession has been fulfilled for that matter.

Praying For The Saints

Chapter Eight

rayer is an essential ingredient in the fulfilment of God's Word and His will in your life as a Christian, and you need to be constantly mindful of its importance.

I've seen folks who have been Christians for many years, but rather than grow spiritually, they grew more and more religious. They emphasized how long they'd been Christians, and prided themselves in their long stay in the faith. God's

Word and the things of the Spirit became so commonplace to them, because they thought they'd seen and heard it all. Such an attitude is offensive to the Spirit of God.

This is why we ought to pray for the saints of God, so that they'll know His Word by revelation and be effective in the things of the Spirit.

Wisdom and Revelation

"Wherefore I also, after I heard of your faith in the Lord Jesus, and love unto all the saints, Cease not to give thanks for you, making mention of you in my prayers; That the God of our Lord Jesus Christ, the Father of glory, may give unto you the spirit of wisdom and revelation in the knowledge of him: The eyes of your understanding being enlightened; that ye may know what is the hope of his

calling, and what the riches of the
glory of his inheritance in the saints,
And what is the exceeding greatness
of his power to us-ward who
believe..." (Ephesians 1:15-19).

You may confess, "I have the spirit of wisdom and revelation," but it doesn't come just by confession; otherwise Paul wouldn't have had to pray this prayer for the Ephesian Christians.

The spirit of wisdom Paul talked about here is the same mentioned in **Isaiah 11:1-2:**

"And there shall come forth a rod out
of the stem of Jesse, and a Branch
shall grow out of his roots: And the
spirit of the LORD shall rest upon him,
the spirit of wisdom and understanding,
the spirit of counsel and might, the
spirit of knowledge and of the fear of
the LORD;"

Paul said, *"I pray that God may give you the spirit of wisdom and revelation in the knowledge of him (God)."* This is an intercession Paul made on behalf of the Ephesian Christians.

Now, there are people who are born again, who have come to accept that God is their heavenly Father, Jesus is the Son of God, and the Holy Spirit is the third Person of the Godhead, but they don't have divine insights about God. They've received the Holy Spirit, but haven't come to know the kind of heavenly Father they have, or who the Holy Spirit is and what He can do in their lives.

You ought to intercede for such people who have been born again but don't have the light of God's Word. They may even be 'old' Christians, but as long as they're not walking in the light of God's Word, they should be prayed for in this manner.

You can also personalize the Pauline prayer

in the book of Ephesians to yourself, for increase of revelation and wisdom. The Bible talked about how Jesus grew in wisdom and stature and in favor with God and men (Luke 2:52). When you pray this way for yourself, you'll also begin to experience spiritual development and have insight into the things of God.

The Knowledge of God's Will

"For this cause we also, since the day we heard it, do not cease to pray for you, and to desire that ye might be filled with the knowledge of his will in all wisdom and spiritual understanding;" (Colossians 1:9).

We need to apply wisdom and spiritual understanding in our lives. The Lord Jesus functioned by them; that's why He could fulfil His ministry on earth in spite of the criticisms and persecutions He faced.

When the Pharisees asked His views on the payment of taxes, He took a piece of coin and asked, "Whose image is on it?"

"Caesar's," they answered.

Then He said, *"Give unto Caesar what is Caesar's and unto God what is God's,"* (Matthew 22:21) and they were all dumbfounded.

That was wisdom! When you study the life of Jesus and how He responded to the constant baiting from the Pharisees, Sadducees, scribes, and doctors of the law, you can't but agree that He really is the embodiment of Wisdom.

By operating in wisdom, Jesus also knew when to escape from physical harm, even though He was the all-powerful Son of God. On a certain occasion, He had just finished preaching in the temple court when some of the Jews, offended by His teaching, wanted to seize Him and stone Him to death. He knew it wasn't yet His time to be offered up, because

He had spiritual understanding of the mind of God, and so He escaped before they could capture Him (John 10:22-39).

Some Christians in the same situation today could say, "Nobody can touch me!" or "Go ahead and shoot; it won't hurt me!" Meanwhile, the Spirit of Wisdom could be telling them to get out of there. This may have been what happened with Paul that he was beaten to death at one time in Lystra. Thank God for the prayers of the saints that brought him back to life (Acts 14:19-20). Of course, we must also remember that the Lord said we would suffer persecution for His sake. Therefore, we're not exempt from such experiences either. Nevertheless, the Lord would have us filled with the knowledge of His will in all wisdom and spiritual understanding. I believe in this kind of prayer, and I have prayed it for myself and others through the years.

The Spirit of Might

"That he would grant you, according to the riches of his glory, to be strengthened with might by his Spirit in the inner man;"(Ephesians 3:16).

Colossians 1:11 also says:

"Strengthened with all might, according to his glorious power, unto all patience and longsuffering with joyfulness."

Here we see Paul praying for the Ephesian and Colossian Christians to be strengthened with might. 'Might' here is not referring to your muscles or physical strength. It refers to the miracle-working ability of God through the Spirit.

Remember that in Acts 1:8, Jesus said to His disciples, *"Ye shall receive **power** after that the Holy Ghost is come upon you."* The word *"power"* in Acts 1:8 is from the same Greek word "dunamis" translated "might" in Ephesians 3:16

and Colossians 1:11.

Power is the inherent, dynamic ability to cause changes. If you want changes in your body, family, job, or finances, you received the inherent, dynamic ability to effect those changes when you received the Holy Ghost!

Thus, "might" in Ephesians 3:16 connotes miracle-working ability. So Paul's prayer is that we be invigorated with miracle-working power in our spirits by the Holy Ghost.

When this ability of the Spirit came upon Samson, it made Him more than a man and he performed extraordinary feats. One day, he got to the city gate of Gaza and pulled it out, poles, bars and all! You can imagine how heavy a city gate could be. Well, Samson not only pulled this one out, he hefted it on his shoulder and carried it far away from town to the top of a hill! That's might!

But Samson did even more. After the

Philistines had captured him and gouged his eyes, they brought him out to entertain them during a great feast they were having in the temple of Dagon. Then Samson prayed, *"O Lord God, remember me, I pray thee, and strengthen me, I pray thee, only this once, O God, that I may be at once avenged of the Philistines for my two eyes"* (Judges 16:28). After he had prayed thus, the Spirit of might came upon him and gave him superhuman strength as before.

When he placed his hands on the two middle pillars of the temple and started heaving against them, his captors thought he was kidding and started laughing at him. But before they knew what was happening, huge slabs of rock started pelting down as the supporting columns gave way. Their laughter turned into screams of terror as they were crushed under the huge stones that fell from everywhere in the building.

Samson brought the whole building down on over three thousand people and not one of them escaped; he killed more Philistines in his death than in his lifetime. He was indeed a mighty man of valour, the champion of Israel.

David must have read about Samson and was inspired by his testimonies. The day came when Samuel, the prophet of God, poured oil on David's head and anointed him as king. From then on, the Spirit of the Lord rested upon David. He went back to tending his father's sheep, but he was a different man; he was carrying the anointing.

One of those days, a lion came to take a lamb from his flock. Other men would have fled, but David, anointed by the Spirit of might, charged after the lion, caught it by its beard and killed it, and delivered the lamb from its mouth.

Another time, a bear came to take one of the lambs and it met the same fate as the lion.

Also, when he faced Goliath of Gath, the Philistine giant, he told him he would end up like those beasts he had killed, and that was exactly what happened.

These acts of magnificent gallantry were not done in Samson's or David's physical strength, but by the anointing of the Spirit of might that came upon them.

When the Spirit of might is at work in you, He not only gives you boldness, but also brings you might—that overpowering force or extraordinary power that overcomes and surpasses strength itself.

This is why you've got to pray, not only for yourself but for other saints also, that we be filled with the Spirit of might to do superhuman things and bring glory to the Lord.

Christ In Our Hearts

The Spirit of God at several times inspired Paul and other apostles of the early Church to pray for the saints. One of such instructive prayers is found in **Ephesians 3:14-17:**

> *"For this cause I bow my knees unto the Father of our Lord Jesus Christ, Of whom the whole family in heaven and earth is named, That he would grant you, according to the riches of his glory, to be strengthened with might by his Spirit in the inner man; That Christ may dwell in your hearts by faith..."*

Here, Paul prays for God's people that Christ may dwell in our hearts by faith. In other words, he prayed that we'd have a revelation of the mystery of Christ. In Colossians 1:27, he said, *"...God would make known what is the riches of the glory of this mystery among the Gentiles;*

which is Christ in you, the hope of glory:"

Christ in you—this is the mystery that had been hidden for ages and generations. Even the great apostles of Jesus Christ at the council in Jerusalem didn't have a full grasp of it, because until the Holy Spirit taught them differently, they argued that Gentiles couldn't be saved except they were circumcised according to the Old Testament Law (Acts 15:1-2).

The Church of Jesus Christ at that time was still a baby Church. They were just beginning to understand a few things about the resurrection of Jesus Christ and His intercessory ministry for the saints. They didn't realize that Gentiles (non-Jews) too could be saved by the blood of Jesus and become members of His Body. That's why Paul had to pray for them that Christ may dwell in their hearts by faith; that they would understand "this mystery among the Gentiles; which is Christ in you, the hope of glory:"

The Love of Christ

"... that ye, being rooted and grounded in love, May be able to comprehend with all saints what is the breadth, and length, and depth, and height; And to know the love of Christ, which passeth knowledge, that ye might be filled with all the fulness of God" (Ephesians 3:17-19).

This prayer has to do with the revelation of the love of God in our daily walk. We've got to know the length, breadth, height and depth of the compelling love that made the Lord Jesus suffer and die for us.

Have you heard someone say, "I can't please you and displease myself." That's not God's kind of love; folks with such understanding haven't received insight into the mind and plans of God. They're not yet filled with the love of God. This is why you've got to pray for

God's people that they would have insight into the love of Christ, which is beyond natural, human comprehension.

Utterance and Boldness

In Paul's letter to the Ephesian Christians, he asked them to pray for him *"...that utterance may be given unto me, that I may open my mouth boldly, to make known the mystery of the gospel,"* (Ephesians 6:19). In another letter to Timothy, he said, *"...God has not given us a spirit of fear (cowardice, timidity), but of power and of love and of a sound mind"* (2 Timothy 1:7 NKJV).

All these show that God wants His children to be very courageous. Paul asked the saints to intercede for him so he would be able to open his mouth boldly to preach the gospel, not because he didn't have the spirit of boldness. Certainly not! Remember, it was Paul himself who affirmed that God hasn't given us a spirit of fear, but one of power, love, and a sound mind.

Imagine if a child of God gets the chance to face a crowd and share the gospel, and suddenly gets nervous. If the boldness of God doesn't rise from his spirit, he'll likely lose that wonderful opportunity to bring many to salvation. So when you pray like this for God's saints, what you're asking is for that character of God that is expressed in love, boldness, power, and wisdom to be evident in their lives.

That Love May Abound

"And this I pray, that your love may abound yet more and more in knowledge and in all judgment; That ye may approve things that are excellent; that ye may be sincere and without offence till the day of Christ; Being filled with the fruits of righteousness, which are by Jesus

Christ, unto the glory and praise of God" (Philippians 1:9-11).

I love Paul; he prayed with knowledge and understanding. He prayed, "that your love may abound yet more and more in knowledge." Love with knowledge is vital. He also prayed that our love will be in all judgment, that is, through the Spirit of counsel within, our love will be displayed with a good sense of judgment. Judgment here doesn't refer to the kind handed down by a judge in a courtroom, but the ability to walk with divine counsel and know what to do by spiritual intuition.

Paul also prayed that the Holy Spirit would work in our lives and enable us to approve things that are excellent, being filled with the fruits of righteousness.

These are just some of the many prayers you can pray for God's people to build them up, strengthen them and cause His counsel to be established in their lives. So it's time for you to make a fresh commitment to your intercessory ministry. Your motivation for intercession is not to see God meet your personal needs, but to see His will established in the lives of others. There's so much you can accomplish when you pray like this. So, get to work. Start interceding for others and expect positive changes and outstanding results.

Praying For Material Needs

Chapter Nine

ather, give me a house." "Lord, please give me a car." "Oh God, I need some money." "I need a new job." The list of things you genuinely need or want in life could go on endlessly, but do you realize you shouldn't pray such 'give-me' prayers anymore? That's because all things are yours already. That's what the Word says in **1 Corinthians 3:21-23**:

"Therefore let no man glory in men.

For all things are yours; Whether Paul,
or Apollos, or Cephas, or the world,
or life, or death, or things present, or
things to come; all are yours; And ye
are Christ's; and Christ is God's."

You may be wondering, "How then am I supposed to have and enjoy all these things if I don't pray and ask God for them?"

That's what I'll be showing you in this chapter, for God's Word reveals to us how to receive our material needs.

My God Shall Supply All Your Need!

The first thing you need to establish concerning your needs is that God is more willing to meet them than you're willing to receive them. This is why Jesus said it's not right for us to make vain repetitions when we pray (Matthew 6:7).

Paul said in Philippians 2:13 that *"it is God*

who works in you both to will and to do for His good pleasure" (NKJV). John, speaking the mind of God, also said, "Beloved, I wish above all things that thou mayest prosper and be in health, even as thy soul prospereth" (3 John 1:2). This proves that your desire for good things is a reflection of God's desire for you.

Paul made a profound statement to the Philippians concerning their needs, which is very applicable to us today. He said, "But my God shall supply all your need according to his riches in glory by Christ Jesus" (Philippians 4:19).

Was Paul talking about their spiritual needs or could he have been referring to their material needs at this instance? We'll find out as we study this scripture in context.

> "Now ye Philippians know also, that
> in the beginning of the gospel, when I
> departed from Macedonia, no church
> communicated with me as concerning

giving and receiving, but ye only. For
even in Thessalonica ye sent once and
again unto my necessity" (Philippians
4:15-16).

Now, Paul remarked that no other church
had communicated with him concerning giving
and receiving except the Philippian church,
meaning he must have received some material
things from them. It was on that premise,
therefore, that he said in verse 19: *"But my God*
shall supply all your need according to his riches
in glory by Christ Jesus."

"Supply" here doesn't merely connote
provision; it's translated from the Greek word
"pleroo," which means "to make replete or
surplus." Paul is therefore letting us know that
God's plan is not just to meet our needs but to
make them available in surplus, that is, in
quantities much larger than desired or required.

When Paul said, *"My God shall supply all*
your need," he wasn't making a promise on

God's behalf, nor was he giving us a promise from God. It may sound like a promise, but it's not. If it had been written: "The Lord said, 'I shall supply your need according to My riches in glory,'" then we could take it as a promise from God. But Paul wrote: "My God shall supply all your need according to His riches in glory by Christ Jesus." This is a statement of fact that lets us know God's role in the contract. It means that the moment you recognize a need, it is lined up with God's supply system. Therefore, you shouldn't be praying about your needs because the Word already declares that they're supplied according to God's riches in glory by Christ Jesus.

If your rent is due, for example, you shouldn't pray, "Oh God, please help me; I need to pay my rent." That wouldn't do it. What you ought to do is declare, "I have my needs met according to God's riches in glory by Christ Jesus. Therefore, in the Name of Jesus, I receive money for my rent!"

As a matter of fact, you ought to declare this long before your rent is due. This doesn't mean that God might be caught unawares if you don't. But when you declare the Word earlier, you have time to strengthen your faith and prevent panic.

Now, you don't make such faith-declarations just because that's what you're expected to do, but because you believe them absolutely. Paul declared in 2 Corinthians 4:13, *"We having the same spirit of faith, according as it is written, I believed, and therefore have I spoken; we also believe, and therefore speak."* You also believe, and that's why you speak!

Voice The Supply, Not The Need!

Be "supply-conscious" and not "need-conscious." There're certain things that God has worked out for your good that you probably don't know about. Yet there're other things that come into your consciousness and you realize you have a need. After identifying a need like that, don't start praying and asking God to meet that need. Don't make it the focus of your prayer. If you do, you'll be voicing your need instead of your supply.

What you should do is declare that God has supplied that need. You say, "Father, in the Name of Jesus, I receive my house." When you do that, you connect to God's supply system. It does sound too simple, but that's the gospel. That's what the Good News is all about. It's so easy, you don't have to struggle or beg. When the things you want aren't covered by the gospel, you'll have to fast, strive, and pay the price for them. But when they fall within the provisions of Christ's glorious gospel, you can relax, knowing they're yours already.

It's No Longer "Give Us This Day Our Daily Bread"

Jesus taught His disciples to pray to the Father, *"Give us this day our daily bread"* (Matthew 6:11). This prayer was necessary at the time because, through Adam, man had lost control over the earth when he committed high treason and gave Satan dominion over it. That's why man had to pray for his daily bread, because Satan had set up an evil system that was in control of the world. This went on until Jesus came, whipped the devil, and gained the mastery.

You see, there's a huge difference between the life of the Old Testament and that of the new creation in Christ.   In the Old Testament, the Jews had to pray and ask God for their daily bread. They had to ask Him to meet their every need. Jesus taught them to pray that way before He died. But His death, burial, resurrection and ascension have ushered in a new dispensation. In this new order, we don't pray like the Old Testament Jews. As new creations in Christ, we've been vested with all His power and authority to call forth and to receive what we desire.

In Matthew 28:18-20, Jesus said, *"...All power is given unto me in heaven and in earth. Go ye therefore and teach all nations, baptizing them in the name of the Father, and of the Son, and of the Holy Ghost: Teaching them to observe all things whatsoever I have commanded you: and, lo, I am with you alway, even unto the end of the world. Amen."*

Now, in His Name, we rule over the principalities and powers of darkness and we have our needs met. We don't have to ask God, "Give us this day our daily bread." We simply claim our daily bread, because it's ours already! We don't ask now for our needs to be met; we declare that they're met.

Matthew 11:28-30:

"Come unto me, all ye that labour and are heavy laden, and I will give you rest. Take my yoke upon you, and learn of me; for I am meek and lowly in heart: and ye shall find rest unto your souls. For my yoke is easy, and my burden is light."

Jesus is saying here, "Let Me be Lord of your life. 'Lord,' in the New Testament, doesn't only mean *boss*; it also connotes *bread-provider*, *protector* and *caretaker*.

He also says to you, "Take My yoke upon you for My yoke is easy and my burden is light." He is letting you know that the way He leads you is very simple. The responsibilities that He gives you are very light and easy. John the apostle says His commandments are not grievous (1 John 5:3); the simplicity of the gospel is proof it came from God.

Think about it, how were all the sins you had committed since birth forgiven? As numerous and terrible as they were, all you had to say was, "I receive Jesus as Lord of my life," and they were all gone from your life in an instant, just like that!

If it was that simple for you to receive eternal life, then you've got to agree that life in the Kingdom is that way too. So, refuse to live a life of failure; don't even allow its consciousness in your heart or mind.

You Shall Lay Up Gold As Dust!

"Then shalt thou lay up gold as dust, and the gold of Ophir as the stones of the brooks. Yea, the Almighty shall be thy defence, and thou shalt have plenty of silver" (Job 22:24-25).

To lay up gold as dust means your supply

never ends. When you wipe a surface clean of dust and give some time, it won't be long before some dust finds its way back there. This Scripture above is letting you know that's how money will keep coming to you. It may be the beginning of a month and you're about to use up your last cash. Don't start fretting and wondering what you're going to do. Don't reason: "*Where should I expect money to come from? I only have one source—my monthly paycheck!*" Don't talk like that. That's the world's way of talking. That's the way the world's system operates. Your job or business is not your source; God is your source!

Here's what you should do instead: declare, "I lay up gold as dust, in the Name of Jesus!

You can't be in God's Kingdom and talk the language of the world. Don't conform yourself to the way the world reasons and talks. Be transformed by the renewing of your mind; train yourself to think and talk according to the Word of God!

Don't Stay In "The Finishing Process"

Make up your mind that you're not going to be lack-conscious but supply-conscious. When you're always making statements like, "Things are tight. I have to manage. If I give or spend so much, I won't have anything left," you're inadvertently bringing yourself to a position of disadvantage. That's lack-consciousness. If you keep thinking like that, you're in 'The Finishing Process,' where everything trickles down to a zero.

Let me be quick to indicate here that your spending and giving must be for the right purpose. When the furtherance of the gospel is your priority, angels will always be on assignment for you, literally working overtime to ensure you never lack, simply because you've made God's business your business and His concerns yours. He'll see to it that your needs are met always!

God wants you to begin operating at that higher level of spiritual consciousness where your spiritual eyes are open to see that the world belongs to you. As you consciously develop yourself in God's Word, you'll realize many of your prayer requests are not necessary, because He's already given you everything that pertains to life and godliness. At that level, much of your prayers become confessions, decrees, pronouncements, worship and thanksgiving.

You can lay claims to your possessions by walking in the light of God's Word. This means you walk in the practical consciousness of what the Word says about your Kingdom rights, privileges, and possessions in Christ Jesus. Part of this is a continual confession of God's Word. Recognize that the Christian life is a life of confession (Romans 10:8-10; Hebrews 3:1). The

Bible says, *"Death and life are in the power of the tongue: and they that love it shall eat the fruit thereof"* (Proverbs 18:21). So your confession matters a great deal. If you say you're broke, that's contrary to what the Word of God says concerning you in Psalm 23:1: *"The Lord is my shepherd; I shall not want."*

Walk in the light of the Word. Declare: *"The Lord is my shepherd; therefore, I refuse to lack. I'm a big-time financier of the gospel. Doors of opportunity are open unto me right now. I am blessed and all my needs are abundantly supplied according to God's riches in glory by Christ Jesus, Hallelujah!"*

Prophetic Prayer

Chapter Ten

*P*rophetic prayer refers to the prayer in which you speak the will and purpose of God into being by the divine inspiration of the Holy Spirit.

When you worship the Lord in Spirit and in truth in the place of prayer, the Holy Spirit causes His Word to come forth from you with power and authority.

A classic example of prophetic prayer is

Jonah's prayer to God when he was in the belly of the fish.

> *"Then Jonah prayed unto the LORD his God out of the fish's belly, And said, I cried by reason of mine affliction unto the LORD, and he heard me; out of the belly of hell cried I, and thou heardest my voice. For thou hadst cast me into the deep, in the midst of the seas; and the floods compassed me about: all thy billows and thy waves passed over me. Then I said, I am cast out of thy sight; yet I will look again toward thy holy temple" (Jonah 2:1-4).*

Jonah was as good as dead, but in his hour of desperation in the fish's belly, he refused to give up. Instead, he called upon God, because he wanted to see His glory again. He wanted to see Jerusalem again, the city of the great King, where the temple of God was.

Jonah understood perfectly what he was doing. He was in a terribly hopeless situation, but then he prophesied: "I will look again toward thy holy temple!"

This is prophetic prayer, and it's important for the believer to pray this way. In prophetic prayer, you put to work the gift of prophecy by which you speak forth the mind of the Father. You speak the will of God into being by the inspiration of the Holy Ghost, and it becomes.

Refuse To Observe Lying Vanities

"When my soul fainted within me I remembered the Lord; and my prayer came in unto thee, into thine holy temple. They that observe lying vanities forsake their own mercy" (Jonah 2:7-8).

You may read this and think, *Oh, well,*

Jonah said this after he came out from the fish's belly. No, he didn't. He spoke it while still in the belly of the fish. He said those that observe lying vanities forsake their mercies. He knew that looking at the circumstances would make him forsake the mercies of God. He had come to realize that God loved him more than he loved himself; God cared more about his reputation than he ever could. Jonah had come to terms with the Spirit of God, so he refused to dwell on his distressing circumstances, and while still in trouble, he began to thank God for delivering him.

Jonah didn't say, "God, I know you'll deliver me." Rather, he said, "You delivered me." It takes faith to talk like that. In prophetic prayer, you speak the past tense of God's Word. You don't say, "I'm going to be healed," or "God's going to heal me" or "I claim my healing." You declare, "I've been healed! Thank you, Lord, for healing me!" Glory to God!

Jonah declared that he'd give God sacrifices of thanksgiving. He wasn't thanking God in advance, with the hope that God would then do what he'd thanked Him for. He was a prophet of God and he understood the Word of God. He knew God calls things that be not as though they were (Romans 4:17).

You're yet to see tomorrow, but God sees and knows your tomorrow. To Him, your tomorrow is already in the past. He's not planning for it, for He's already done all that needs to be done about it. What a comfort to know you serve the living God who knows your future and has made adequate preparations for it!

Don't ever be moved by the unpleasantness of your present circumstances; don't observe those negative symptoms of ill-health. Jonah considered his gloomy circumstances as lying vanities.

If you walk according to your feelings, you'll

only praise God when you feel good; and when you feel otherwise, you conclude that He's forsaken you. As a child of God, you shouldn't walk according to your feelings or circumstances. Refuse to observe lying vanities; instead, hold on to what God has said.

Turn Your Trial Into Triumphant Praise

Jonah turned the fish's belly into a temple and had church right there! He made up his mind not to wallow in self-pity but to give sacrifices of praise to God with the voice of thanksgiving. As he did, the sweet-smelling savour of his sacrifice ascended to God. God was moved by it and spoke to the fish to let Jonah go. It responded and vomited Jonah on dry ground. The same way God spoke to that fish and it responded, He can speak to any circumstance that seems to have swallowed you and it will surely respond.

You simply need to do as Jonah did—begin to worship God in the midst of any seemingly hopeless situation you may have gotten into. Declare that you have overcome; thank Him for your deliverance and victory. These prophetic utterances will bring about the miracle you require and prod you towards fulfilling God's purpose for your life. That's the power of prophetic prayer.

The Prayer of Worship, Praise, and Thanksgiving

Chapter Eleven

The highest call of the believer is the call to fellowship with God, and along with this great call comes the priestly ministry.

> *"And hath made us kings and priests unto God and his Father; to him be glory and dominion forever and ever. Amen"* *(Revelation 1:6).*

As priests of God, we have an important

function in the Body of Christ, and it's necessary for us to examine how the Old Testament priests operated in order for us to better understand our own role as New Testament priests of God, for the priestly office of the Old Testament typifies the priestly ministry of the believer today.

The Outer Court And The Altar Of Brass

The temple of the Old Testament was partitioned into three sections:

- **The Outer Court**

- **The Inner Court**

- **The Holy of Holies, that is, the holiest place of all**

In the outer court was a wooden altar overlaid with brass, symbolizing judgment. The sacrifice of brass, also known as the evening sacrifice, was the burnt offering of the lamb on the altar of brass. It meant that the sins of the people had been placed on the lamb and judged. That's the reason the Psalmist cried out, *"Let my prayer be set forth before thee as incense; and the lifting up of my hands as the evening sacrifice"* (Psalm 141:2).

When David wrote this Psalm he was well-acquainted with the priestly ministry of the Old Testament, and, because he was a prophet of God, he had a revelation of the new dispensation that should follow after the death and resurrection of Jesus Christ. The anointing upon him gave him insight into the heart of God. So he spoke prophetically and likened the evening sacrifice (the sacrifice of brass) to the lifting of hands in worship.

When your hands are lifted up in worship, you're declaring that you've accepted the judgment of the Lamb of God—Jesus Christ—for your sins and have yielded to Him. No sin can condemn you when your hands are lifted up with this consciousness.

The Inner Court And The Altar Of Gold

In the inner court of the Old Testament tabernacle, also known as the first sanctuary or the holy place, there was another wooden altar overlaid with gold. This second altar was right before the great curtain that separated the holy place from the most holy place, and here, the high priest burnt incense every morning and evening, perpetually (Exodus 30:1-8). This was a special rite performed by the High Priest just before he entered the presence of God in the most holy place.

David's statement about his prayer coming to God as incense (Psalm 141:2) referred to the incense on the altar of gold. David looked into the future by the inspiration of the Holy Spirit and saw a new ministry where the priests no longer needed to burn incense every morning and offer lambs every evening. The prayers of God's people, and the lifting up of their hands would be even more pleasing to God.

Psalm 69:30-31:

"I will praise the name of God with a song, and will magnify him with thanksgiving. This also shall please the Lord better than an ox or bullock that hath horns and hoofs."

In David's day, the priest and the people had to offer sacrifices of bulls and goats, but David knew by revelation that there was something more. So he wrote in this psalm that worshipping, praising, and giving God thanks please Him more than the sacrifices of bulls and goats.

The same revelation was shared by another Old Testament prophet, albeit in different words.

Hosea 14:1-2:

"O Israel, return unto the Lord thy

> *God; for thou hast fallen by thine*
> *iniquity. Take with you words, and*
> *turn to the Lord: say unto him, Take*
> *away all iniquity, and receive us*
> *graciously: so will we render the*
> *calves of our lips."*

Bless God, the calves of our lips! What a revelation!

Lifting Holy Hands Brings Victory

How important the lifting of your hands is to God! When you lift up your hands, it's not just a sign of worship; it's a ministry! It's the most beautiful thing to behold when God's people lift their hands to Him in worship. As you speak forth words of praise to God and lift up your hands to heaven, you're sending incense of a sweet-smelling savour to Him. The lifting up of your hands has taken the place of the burnt sacrifice, and your prayers, the burning incense. When your hands are lifted up, that's the time to adore and thank the Lord; the time to worship Him, not a time to beg and cry. It's the time to make a sacrifice of joy that springs from a heart full of love and thanksgiving.

Every time a minister tells you to lift your hands in worship, don't get tired and put your hands down so quickly. Moses found out there's something powerful about lifting your hands. It wasn't written in the Law, but he discovered it! Let's read his discovery:

> *"And Moses said unto Joshua, Choose us out men, and go out, fight with Amalek: to morrow I will stand on the top of the hill with the rod of God in mine hand. So Joshua did as Moses had said to him, and fought with Amalek: and Moses, Aaron, and Hur went up to the top of the hill. And it came to pass, when Moses held up his*

hand, that Israel prevailed: and when
he let down his hand, Amalek
prevailed. But Moses' hands were
heavy; and they took a stone, and put
it under him, and he sat thereon; and
Aaron and Hur stayed up his hands,
the one on the one side, and the other
on the other side; and his hands were
steady until the going down of the sun"
(Exodus 17:9-12).

How remarkable and instructive! Now, the Lord didn't command Moses to lift up his hands when he got to the top of that hill, but he, Aaron, and Hur observed that whenever he lifted his hands, Israel prevailed, but as soon as his hands came down, Israel began to lose. So the two men got Moses a stone to sit on and held up both his hands. And as long as Moses' hands were held up, Israel prevailed.

Paul also understood the importance of lifting our hands, so he charged us in 1 Timothy

2:8, *"I will therefore that men pray every where, lifting up holy hands without wrath and doubting."*

If you've been going through difficulties in your life that don't seem to go away, maybe this is what you haven't done yet. When you pray with your hands lifted up, it's a signal of victory in the realm of the spirit, and you will prevail over that situation and have the victory, glory to God!

Worship In The New Testament

"But the hour cometh, and now is, when the true worshippers shall worship the Father in spirit and in truth: for the Father seeketh such to worship him" (John 4:23).

Worship is a vital part of the priestly ministry of the believer. It held a prominent role in the Old Testament and still does today.

It's one thing to worship God, and another thing to worship Him the right way. That you feel good while worshipping doesn't mean you're worshipping right, just as eating junk and feeling good about it doesn't mean you're eating right. So it's not about the feeling you get; you must be sure you're worshipping God God's way as shown in His Word.

In John 4:23, Jesus outlined the characteristics of true worshippers: they worship the Father **in spirit** and **in truth**. Now, this doesn't necessarily mean singing softly and slowly; it connotes worshipping God from your spirit and according to His Word.

There must be a union of your spirit with God's Spirit in order to serve and worship Him. This means you must be born again and filled with the Holy Spirit to be able to worship God in spirit and in truth. Paul said, *"God is my witness, whom I serve with my spirit in the gospel of his Son..."* (Romans 1:9).

When you worship God in Spirit and in reality, there's a union and drinking together of spirits. It is called the communion of the Holy Spirit. It isn't just in our singing or in the words of our prayer, but in the communication and transportation that take place in the realm of the spirit. Worship transports you to lofty divine realms. This is why you feel enraptured as you worship sometimes; it's as though you're taken away from the earth realm into the warmth of God's Spirit. You find yourself completely oblivious of everyone and everything around you as God's glorious presence envelopes you.

The Sacrifice of Praise and Thanksgiving

The Bible says, *"By him (Jesus Christ) therefore let us offer the sacrifice of praise to God continually, that is, the fruit of our lips giving thanks to his name"* (Hebrews 13:15).

Just as the priest offered sacrifices of burnt

offerings and incense in the Old Testament, today we offer sacrifices of praise to God with the fruit of our lips, which are the words we speak in praise and thanksgiving to the Lord.

The sacrifice of praise transcends superficial statements like, "Lord, I thank you for everything." For it to be praise, it must be mixed with substance from your spirit. When you give God thanks, you must have definite reasons for doing so, and when you voice those reasons, that's praise!

If I said, "Thank you for sweeping this place," I have praised you. Therefore, praising God means giving Him thanks in the Name of Jesus for specific reasons. The sacrifices of praise are confessions, declarations, psalms, hymns, and spiritual songs that you render to God for His grace and goodness. They also refer to tributes or speeches that acknowledge and celebrate the Name of the Lord. They are confessions of God's Word that we make to glorify Him. These confessions (or professions) are the fruits and calves of our lips, words from our mouths that give glory to God. So when you're making confessions, say beautiful things about God and give testimonies of His wondrous works. Proclaim what God has said about Himself and about you. As you make those confessions in Jesus' Name, He (Jesus) as our Great High Priest presents them before the Father, who receives your praise and worship as a sacrifice of a sweet-smelling savour, Hallelujah!

Learn To Activate The Power

You may be faced with a difficult situation today that you've prayed and cried out to God about. You may even have confessed that it's all working out for your good. All that is beautiful, but if you want things to change, then it's time you took this step I'm about to show you.

You see, as Christians, God hears and

answers us when we pray, but how to make His power that is released in our behalf work for us is what many don't know. One of the ways to activate that power is through praise! Throughout the scriptures, there're amazing and inspiring accounts of how God delivered His people from certain destruction when they activated His power through praise. Let's look at a few of them.

Put The Singers In Front!

Three nations—Ammon, Moab, and Mount Seir—came out against Judah and made ready to attack her. The Bible tells us that Jehoshaphat, the King of Judah at the time prayed to God and said, "Oh God, you gave us this land, and now these people want to take it from us and drive us out of it" (2 Chronicles 20:6-11).

You see, just because God gave you something, doesn't mean the devil will not try to take it away from you. Satan tried through

Ammon, Moab and Mount Seir to take from the children of Judah the land God had given them. But King Jehoshaphat was wise. He gathered all Judah together to seek the Lord in prayer and fasting. When they prayed, God spoke to them through Jahaziel, one of the sons of the prophets.

2 Chronicles 20:14-19:

"Then upon Jahaziel the son of Zechariah, the son of Benaiah, the son of Jeiel, the son of Mattaniah, a Levite of the sons of Asaph, came the Spirit of the Lord in the midst of the congregation; And he said, Hearken ye, all Judah, and ye inhabitants of Jerusalem, and thou king Jehoshaphat, Thus saith the Lord unto you, Be not afraid nor dismayed by reason of this great multitude; for the battle is not yours, but God's. To morrow go ye down against them:

behold, they come up by the cliff of Ziz; and ye shall find them at the end of the brook, before the wilderness of Jeruel. Ye shall not need to fight in this battle: set yourselves, stand ye still, and see the salvation of the Lord with you, O Judah and Jerusalem: fear not, nor be dismayed; to morrow go out against them: for the Lord will be with you. And Jehoshaphat bowed his head with his face to the ground: and all Judah and the inhabitants of Jerusalem fell before the Lord, worshipping the Lord. And the Levites, of the children of the Kohathites, and of the children of the Korhites, stood up to praise the Lord God of Israel with a loud voice on high."

God gave Jehoshaphat and the children of Israel the exact location of their enemies' camp, and also gave him a strategy to defeat them:

2 Chronicles 20:21:

"And when he had consulted with the people, he appointed singers unto the Lord, and that should praise the beauty of holiness, as they went out before the army, and to say, Praise the Lord; for his mercy endureth for ever."

Have you ever heard of an army going to war and they put singers at the forefront? It sounds stupid, but that's the strategy God gave Jehoshaphat and that's exactly what he did. Before going out against the enemy, he put singers in front of the army, and they marched towards their enemies' position, singing, "Praise the Lord, for His mercy endureth forever!"

2 Chronicles 20:22 :

"When they began to sing and to praise, the LORD set ambushments against the children of Ammon, Moab,

and mount Seir, which were come
against Judah; and they were smitten."

As the singers went ahead of the army singing and praising God, the Lord set ambushments against the enemy, and they drew their swords on each other and fought and killed one another. By the time Israel's army got to their enemies' camp, they were all dead! They didn't have to lift a finger in battle, much less shed a drop of blood to defeat this mighty army that came out to destroy them.

When trouble strikes, like Jehoshaphat, you can "put the singers in front" and expect to have the same result. At such times, don't wait until you feel like singing before you sing. Make a song of praise and sing, whether you feel like it or not, whether you're happy or not. When the children of Israel discovered they were about to be attacked by the allied forces of Ammon, Moab and Mount Seir, it was far from a happy celebration. All they were happy about as they marched out to face this formidable enemy was that God had spoken to them and told them to praise Him. They did, and God gave them the victory.

A Supernatural Jailbreak

Paul's and Silas' supernatural release from a Roman maximum security prison is another inspiring example of how God's power was activated through praise.

Acts 16:22-26 :

"And the multitude rose up together against them: and the magistrates rent off their clothes, and commanded to beat them. And when they had laid many stripes upon them, they cast them into prison, charging the jailer to keep them safely: Who, having received such a charge, thrust them into the inner prison, and made their

feet fast in the stocks. And at midnight
Paul and Silas prayed, and sang
praises unto God: and the prisoners
heard them. And suddenly there was
a great earthquake, so that the
foundations of the prison were shaken:
and immediately all the doors were
opened, and every one's bands were
loosed."

Some people in that situation would have been singing dirges of pain and regret, but not Paul and Silas; they prayed and sang praises to God! The Bible says as they did, the power of God was activated and there was an earthquake in the prison. All the prisoners' bands were broken, the prison doors flung wide open, and they were set free by the power of God. This miraculous encounter led to the salvation of the prison warden and his entire family.

Acts 16:27-34 :

"And the keeper of the prison awaking out of his sleep, and seeing the prison doors open, he drew out his sword, and would have killed himself, supposing that the prisoners had been fled. But Paul cried with a loud voice, saying, Do thyself no harm: for we are all here. Then he called for a light, and sprang in, and came trembling, and fell down before Paul and Silas, And brought them out, and said, Sirs, what must I do to be saved? And they said, Believe on the Lord Jesus Christ, and thou shalt be saved, and thy house. And they spake unto him the word of the Lord, and to all that were in his house. And he took them the same hour of the night, and washed their stripes; and was baptized, he and all his, straightway. And when he had

brought them into his house, he set
meat before them, and rejoiced,
believing in God with all his house."

Learn to sing praises to God, even in the midst of your troubles and challenges. Speak and sing joyous tongues of praise and thanksgiving, and as you do this, the power of God will move in your behalf, and you'll have a mighty deliverance and see great miracles.

Look At The "Son" And You Won't See The Shadows

A young woman who had been sick for several years and finally been given up to die came into one of our meetings some years ago. While she was seated in the hall, diseased and in pain, there was such glorious worship going on that she thought to herself: This is wonderful. If I ever have the opportunity to worship God in my life, this is it!

At that point she looked away from her sickness and up to God. She worshipped the Lord with all of her heart, in spite of the pain racking her body. Suddenly, she noticed that she was lifting her hands. These were the same hands she couldn't move before. For a moment she thought, *How come my hands are going up?* Then it dawned on her that she'd been healed, and she ran out to give her testimony.

She was just worshipping! What wonderful miracles can take place when you turn away from your problems and look instead to the Lord in worship and praise! Helen Keller rightly said that those who look at the sun do not see the shadows. How true! When you worship God, your heart goes to Him and you don't see the evil around you. Jesus is the Sun of righteousness (Malachi 4:2). If you gaze at Him, your troubles will vanish.

The Canaanite woman whose daughter was

grievously vexed with a devil had to turn away from her problems and worship the Master. When she first came to Him, all her attention was on her problem—her daughter who was vexed with a devil—but the Lord answered her not a word until she worshipped (Matthew 15: 21-28). Thank God she had enough sense to take her eyes off her problems to look upon the Master in worship. It got His attention and she got her miracle.

We read another beautiful account in Luke 7:36-47 about a woman who poured her expensive perfume on Jesus' feet. As its sweet scent pervaded the house, her sacrifice was accepted of God because it was from a heart full of worship; and her many sins were forgiven in a moment. Many generations after, we still read about her and learn from her remarkable act of worship.

You need to know that you're accepted of

God as you speak to God in praise and adoration. There's so much to thank Him for; so learn to lift your hands in worship to Him in acknowledgement of His majesty, not just because you want to ask for something. Learn to constantly glorify Him for who He is.

A Special
Invitation
to Prayer

Conclusion

*E*very Monday, Wednesday, and Friday, I send out prayer points and prophetic words to saints around the world as impressed upon my heart by God's Spirit.

These prayer points and prophecies are posted on **www.yookos.com**, and on each of these days, we spend 15 minutes in prayer at 12:00pm (GMT+1) and 10:00pm (GMT+1).

Millions of Christians the world over have

been motivated and mobilized for prayer and intercession through this unique website, and we've had tremendous testimonies from all parts of the globe.

Visit www.yookos.com today and register. To follow me and receive my posts, go to the "pastorchrislive" page (**www.yookos.com/ pastorchrislive**) and click on the "follow pastorchrislive" button. I look forward to welcoming you to the fastest-growing prayer network in the world, where we make tremendous power available, dynamic in its working.

You can also visit **www.christembassy.org** for more information on our ministry and various opportunities that are available to you to impact your world. God bless you.

To contact the author write:
Pastor Chris Oyakhilome:

United Kingdom:
Christ Embassy Int'l Office
LoveWorld Conference Center
Cheriton High Street,
Folkestone, Kent CT19 4QJ
Tel:+44(0)1303 270970
Fax: 01303 274 372

South Africa:
303 Pretoria Avenue
Cnr.Harley and Braam Fischer,
Randburg, Gauteng, South Africa.
Tel: +27-11-326 0971,
+27-11-326 0972

Nigeria:
LoveWorld Conference Center
Kudirat Abiola Way,Oregun, Ikeja,
P.O. Box 13563, Ikeja,
Lagos, Nigeria.
Tel:+234-80233241878
+234-8052464131; +234-1-8925724

or email:pastorchris@christembassy.org
*Please include your testimony or help received from
this book when you write.
Your prayer requests are also welcome.*

PRAYING THE RIGHT WAY

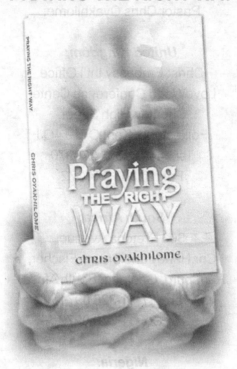

"God wants to answer *ALL* your prayers!
If He had planned it any other way, He would never have
required you to pray. But He'll hear and answer only when
you're 'PRAYING THE RIGHT WAY.'

Discover secrets and principles of effective prayer in
this concise, yet comprehensive book by Chris
Oyakhilome, and rid yourself of any wrong mindsets,
doctrines, perceptions, practices and prayers that may
have clogged the wheels of your prayer life. The
principles are simple, the results guaranteed—a life
full of joy and peace as you receive answers to your
prayers....always.

HOW TO MAKE YOUR FAITH WORK

**Don't get stuck in the rut;
learn how to make your faith work!**

In this outstanding masterpiece, **Pastor Chris**
teaches you not just how to acquire faith, but also
how to put your faith to work so you can live the
life of victory, success, joy, health and, prosperity
that God has planned for you.

HEALING *from*
HEAVEN
Volumes 1&2

...a present-day catalogue of the acts of faith of people who dared to trust God when it seemed all hope was lost, and received miracles and had their health restored.

In them, you'll read touching stories and see telling pictures of hopeless medical conditions turned around through faith in God's Word and His healing anointing. Pastor Chris also shares with you powerful thoughts on faith, healing, miracles, and more.

The "Healing From Heaven" books are undoubtedly requisite for anyone serious about receiving miracle-healing and walking in divine health. But they're not just for the sick; they'll inspire you to trust in the living God for whatever you desire, and show you how to activate your faith for your own miracle!